T0196090

First MEMORY

Multiple Me

SOPHIE MILLER

BALBOA.
PRESS
A DIVISION OF HAY HOUSE

Balboa Press books may be ordered through booksellers or by contacting:

Balboa Press
A Division of Hay House
1663 Liberty Drive
Bloomington, IN 47403
www.balboapress.com
1 (877) 407-4847

Because of the dynamic nature of the Internet, any web addresses or links contained in this book may have changed since publication and may no longer be valid. The views expressed in this work are solely those of the author and do not necessarily reflect the views of the publisher, and the publisher hereby disclaims any responsibility for them.

The author of this book does not dispense medical advice or prescribe the use of any technique as a form of treatment for physical, emotional, or medical problems without the advice of a physician, either directly or indirectly. The intent of the author is only to offer information of a general nature to help you in your quest for emotional and spiritual well-being. In the event you use any of the information in this book for yourself, which is your constitutional right, the author and the publisher assume no responsibility for your actions.

Any people depicted in stock imagery provided by Getty Images are models, and such images are being used for illustrative purposes only.
Certain stock imagery © Getty Images.

Print information available on the last page.

ISBN: 978-1-9822-2035-8 (sc)
ISBN: 978-1-9822-2036-5 (e)

Balboa Press rev. date: 01/24/2019

DEDICATION

This book is dedicated to my friend, "the dragonfly lady" who has always encouraged me to aspire to my potential and to my husband whose love has carried me through it all.

CONTENTS

PREFACE

First Memory is more than the title to this book, it is a concept that I have believed in for quite some time. When events occur in your life that have a powerful impact upon you, you are forever changed. You awaken the next day as a different person for you view things with a new insight and your first conscience thought becomes your first memory for the new you.

I am not saying that each day we are a different person we often go long stretches in sameness, then something happens, that causes you to think or act differently. Once our thoughts or emotional responses shift we are no longer the same we see things from an unfamiliar perspective.

This is my story, the chronological journey of my first memories leading me through a near death experience, a kidnapping, physical, emotional and sexual abuse, angelic intervention, extraterrestrial encounters, joy, despair and growth always growth.

I often felt it was not fair that I had to live through some of the situations I endured in my childhood, but as my spirituality grew I reconciled myself to the choices I made for this lifetime.

It was not easy, fear, anger, hatred, despair, feelings of worthlessness, were my constant companions, but those emotions were not alone, their counterparts of bravery, joy, love, hope, pride were along for the ride too, all aspects of the multiple me.

The hardest yet most rewarding lesson I have learned is forgiveness. If you can't forgive you can't receive, for if all the "bad" stuff remains locked inside you there is no room for the good stuff to occupy.

It is my wish that by inviting you along on my memories journey that you may benefit by it in some way, that your journey will reveal its purpose and you will be able to embrace the magic and Blessings that have been waiting for room in your life.

CHAPTER 1

Rough Start to Life

First memory: Poisoning. The first significant memory in my life occurred just shy of my second birthday. The parts that I remember, though rather vague, are what came to my mind when I heard the story of what happened to me.

I am standing next to a coffee table and I can see in mind's eye my small left hand resting on the table and I am watching my mother polish the furniture. I see her run out of the room then the next image I see is me sitting on my father's right knee and my doll on his left knee. That is all I remember, here is what I was told of the events to fill in the gaps.

My mother was polishing the furniture with Old English furniture oil when she became nauseous from the fumes and ran from the room to vomit as she was several months pregnant with my baby brother. In the moment between my mom leaving the room and my father coming in the room I drank some of the polish.

When my father scooped me up onto his lap he could smell the chemicals on my breath, moments later I passed out. I was rushed to the hospital where they nearly lost me several times. The doctors never told my mother that I had died a couple of times as they feared she would have a miscarriage.

When I recall what little bits of the memory I have, I know I am watching my mother but I only see her and my father from the waist down and I can see the bottle of polish but do not see myself drinking it.

The poisoning created scaring in my lungs, essentially giving me chemical pneumonia. I also suffered kidney damage from it being a petroleum-based product. Throughout my childhood and into my teens I was plagued with bronchitis and kidney infections and had to have chest x-rays every six months then once a year.

It was not until I was in my forties and was channeling that I was given the information that I had, had an NDE (near death experience) at the time of the poisoning. I was reminded when I had my NDE of the difficult path I had chosen for this lifetime and I was shown a beautiful garden where I could mentally retreat to in times of stress.

During the channeling I was told that at the time of the NDE, I had been given a choice to stay in that heavenly realm or go back to my earthly life and continue. Obviously, I chose to come back. All I can say about that decision is that our souls are fearless, enthusiastic and quite possibly brain dead! In the heavenly realm we function on heart not head and it is the lessons for all concerned that matters. With my human mind would I have agreed to come back? On hell, no!

Second memory: Kidnapping. In the summer of my third year I was standing on the front porch of our rental house and I was watching a young man walking down the sidewalk. The man stopped in front of the house and said to me.

"Your mommy says I'm supposed to babysit you."

My response was, "no my mommy is in the house."

While speaking I turn to point at the door and he grabs me from behind and starts running down the sidewalk with me flung over his shoulder and then under his arm, down the hill and across back yards. He finally stops in the back yard of a large white house where there is a lattice enclosure abutting the basement wall.

There is a sloped garden behind me with flowers and I see myself standing there crying hysterically. I am wearing a sundress; my panties are down and he places a penny in the crotch of my underwear. When I spoke of the ordeal of the kidnapping I always relate that he made me sit in an anthill, but I do not recall the image of doing so. I also do not know if he placed the penny before or after he made me sit in the anthill, how long I was gone, or if I was sexually assaulted in any way.

The information about the kidnapping I acquired over the years was that my older brother William, (by one year) went into the house to tell our mother what had happened. I do not remember William being on the porch with me and I don't think the kidnapper could see my brother for I doubt he would have taken me if he had seen him. I am assuming that William may have been down on the floor playing with something.

The police were called and my brother was questioned as to which direction I had been taken. The one humorous aspect of the situation is that my brother, would not tell the officer anything unless he got to hold the officer's gun. Brothers!

Over the years I don't ever remember being told how long I was gone or what happened when I was found, the emphasis on the telling of the story always focused on what a shit my brother had been. Now, when I am most curious about details there is no one to ask. I have no other memories of that house and frankly do not have any tangible memories for about year.

Somewhere between the time of the poisoning and the kidnapping, my parents got divorced and my father took my sister, (who was the oldest and seven years older than me) with him when he left. My sister the sacrificial pawn for the divorce as my mother did not have the resources to fight it.

I think the trauma of my sister being taken away and my father leaving was too great and I just blocked it. I have absolutely no memory of either of them. I would think that at nearly three years old I would have had some recollection of someone who had been in my life daily, but no.

My mom and stepdad got married around the time of my third birthday third, their marriage and the time of the kidnapping back to back.

Before I go any further, I need to divulge the dynamics of my family as it is a vital component in the abusive childhood my brothers and I were about to share. When I was a teenager my mom confided in me all of my father's family's dirty laundry.

My parents' marriage was not a match made in heaven. Mom told me that my father used to beat and rape her, one time so severe that it caused her to miscarry. In order to prevent the attacks my mom thought if she took my sister to bed with her it would prevent him raping her, but to no avail, he just put a pillow over moms' face so her screams would not wake my sister.

When my father was at work, his father, my paternal grandfather, would get drunk and come over to the house and rape her too, threatened with, "who will they believe me or you."

Caught up in this viscous circle my mother became close with my dad's younger brother. Five years younger than her, to my mother he felt harmless, was kind and understanding unlike his brother. They fell in love and also shared a psychic mind link to the point that if she put a thought out to him he would call her. Mom told me that one time when she thought of him he walked two miles to a phone to call her and ask what she wanted. They purposely conspired to have a child together and she knew to the day even the minute she conceived my baby brother.

My stepfather was the youngest of his siblings and had been an unwanted pregnancy, so much so that his mother had tried aborting him several times. My grandparents were party people and liked the bar, even owning one at some point, another child did not fit into their schedule.

As a result of the abortion attempts he was born prematurely and needed extra care, so was given to his aunt and uncle to be raised. My grandmother's sister had been told she could not have children so this seemed the perfect solution although there was no formal adoption. My stepfather was raised by his aunt and uncle, calling them mom and dad and the apple of their eye until at age thirteen or so his "mom" finally became pregnant and again two years later producing two sons. My stepdad went from being number one son to quote his adoptive father, "worthless castoff of his birth mother."

My stepfather's dad/uncle had a fierce temper and could be very brutal. Several of the stories I heard were about his brutality to farm animals. He killed a cow with just a punch of his fist, another by stabbing it with a pitchfork and injured another by twisting its tail off because it kicked him. I'm sure witnessing and being subject to this violence played a major role in my stepdad's future mental stability.

Every few years my paternal grandparents (both sets) would get together with their extended family and close friends for a reunion at a country lodge. This was not your ordinary family reunion but a drunken orgy of wife swapping and debauchery. After a long day of drinking, in the evening, they would all place their room keys in a hat and then each couple would draw a key from the hat to determine whose wife they slept with that night.

Unfortunately, even some of the children were passed around too. This lewd behavior was the legacy of the paternal side of my family for generations, the victims in turn becoming the abusers. I don't think my mother had any inkling of the effect my stepfather's younger life had on his future self, he showed her kindness and love and she truly believed him to be her knight in shining armor, how wrong she was.

Mom and dad (I will refer to my stepdad as dad from here on out as that is what we called him and I have no memory of my biological father) bought a house in the same town in which I was kidnapped, some months after the event. We, my brothers and me always called it, "the brown house" as if it had its own entity and partially because dad had painted the house brown with tan trim. It was there in the brown house that the true terror of my/our childhood began, for my brothers were there alongside me suffering in silence the cruelty and abuse meted out by dad. Not even the fact that my baby brother, was dad's natural son saved him from his share of abuse.

There were a lot of significant memories associated within the brief two years we lived in that house, but there is no particular order I can place them in due to my young age. In fact, there is no memory of anything from the time of the kidnapping until the onset of abuses in the brown house jarred me back to reality. The cruelties started out small but were a daily occurrence and never in the presence of mom.

Third memory: The green carpet. The living room in the brown house was carpeted in a funny, bumpy, textured olive-green carpet. That in and of itself not important but the fact that it generated an enormous amount of static electricity was. Dad would make us kids scuff our feet the full length of the room and then touch the television set so we would get shocked. If we cried or tried not to do it he would yell, kick us and issue dire threats if we didn't do it, and always more threats against us telling mom.

Forth memory: The old lady with the hatchet. This memory haunted my brothers and I for years. Dad had made us watch a horror movie in which a demented old woman with wild grey hair went around splitting people's skulls with a hatchet. The memory of the movie alone would give any small child nightmares but dad insured it would not be forgotten. Dad would play nice in front of mom and offer to tuck us in bed at night and while doing so would whisper in our ears that the old lady with the hatchet would come get us in our beds and that he would laugh while he watched her split our skulls.

I remember getting out of bed after dad left the room and going to sit on the floor under the window in the light of the street lamp trying to stay awake so the old lady with the hatchet wouldn't get me. I'm sure I fell asleep and either mom or dad would place me back in my bed where I would awaken later in full nightmare of the old lady with the hatchet coming to get me. Other nights I would lie awake until I heard my parents go to bed then I would go sit at the top of the stairs, too afraid of my bed and the nightmares awaiting me there. It was there sitting at the top of the stairs that one of my most wonderful memories happened.

Fifth memory: My guardian angel. It started with me in my usual terror sitting on the top step crying when suddenly, I felt this warm love surrounding me, its intensity calming and banishing my fear. I raised my head and looked down at the bottom of the stairwell and there standing in glowing light was the most beautiful being I had ever seen.

The angel had radiant long blond hair and was wearing a shimmering white gown and she looked at me with such love I was mesmerized. She communicated with me not in words but thoughts and told me to trust and believe that everything would work out, that nothing was impossible, to prove this point she asked me to jump down to her and she would catch me. Now mind you I was thirteen steps above her, but I felt no fear and leaped toward her arms. It was not a mad plunge with me falling head over heels down the steps but a slow drift into her waiting arms, her love surrounding me like a warm blanket.

Like any normal child that jumps into someone's arms, my response was, can I do it again? In my excitement to get back up to the top and do it again, it never dawned on me that the first few times I ran back up the stairs I was barely touching the steps, maybe one in every five. Eventually, I was levitating both up and down the stairs until she told me she had to leave and it was time for me to go back to my bed.

This only happened once but it is as fresh to my mind today as it was then. It was many years before I ever heard the word levitation let alone know its meaning, but it was the word I always used in my head when thinking of that night. I firmly believe that my spiritual connections were what enabled me to survive the coming years without completely losing myself.

CHAPTER 2

The Beginning of Hell

By the age of four I began to realize that there was more to this world than most people could see. I had always seen what I referred to as my bubble people. I never mentioned them to anyone for I assumed everyone else saw them too, for they had always been with me. What I saw were shapes that looked like iridescent bubbles interconnected. There were always a few floating around me and when in groups of people their number increased.

What makes this memory so special is that for a few fleeting moments in time two of my bubble people presented themselves in a recognizable physical shape, up until this time the shapes were only geometrical in appearance. Depending on my mood I felt different emotions from them but not words. If I was upset I felt comfort from them and they would gather close. If I was happy they would swirl around me as if dancing.

First memory: Bubble baby. It was the summer I turned four, I was in the backyard, swinging on the swing set, one of my favorite things to do. While I was swinging that day one of my bubble people took the shape of a perfectly formed baby. The bubble baby laid in the curve of my ankles. I was being careful not to let my feet widen too far when I drew them back to push forward and gain momentum so the bubble baby would not fall between my feet. Smiling and humming a tune I swung the "baby Jesus" on my ankles.

I called my mother over from the clothes line to show her I was giving baby Jesus a ride on my ankles. Although mom couldn't see anything, she did not dismiss that I saw something and she asked me about him. I told her he looked like he was made out of bubbles and began pointing at various spots around at other bubble people. Then with a squeal of excitement I pointed off to my right and said, "ooh mommy that one looks like a tiny horse."

The bubble horse I saw was only about twelve inches tall and perfect in form. I only saw the horse the one time but the baby I saw another time, also on a swing, when I was a bit older. Mom told me it was a special gift to see them, I just smiled at her and kept swinging baby Jesus.

I'm sure everyone has seen these little guardians around themselves but may shake it off as an eye floater or hair across the eye. In hospitals and airports, I have counted their numbers in the thousands and they will flock around when I am in situations where emotions are high. I still see them.

Second memory: The closet. Sometime shortly after telling mom about the bubble people we went down to my grandparents' farm, (dad's parents.) Technically, they were his aunt and uncle but to him mom and dad and to my brothers and I grandma and grandpa. I say we all went but do not recall anyone but my cousin in the memory.

My dad's brother/cousin was eight or nine years older than me so it would have made him twelve or thirteen at the time. Taking me by the hand my cousin led me upstairs saying we were going to play a game. Guiding me along he took me through a bedroom and into a large closet. It was not your typical dark, dank closet, more like a small room brightened by a large window. The room was familiar for it was where my grandmother stored games stacked on a tall dark dresser.

My cousin told me to kneel on the floor and taking a box of chess pieces set them on the floor next to me. He proceeded to take a bandana out of his pocket and tie it over my eyes saying as he did so that it was his brother's favorite game. I heard him rattle his hand around in the box of chess pieces and then he brought one to my lips and began pushing it in and out of my mouth. He switched pieces a couple of times and told me not to be surprised if one of them had water in it.

With no warning, the texture changed the next time, hard yet soft and he placed his hand on the back of my head as he moved the object in my mouth. Hearing a sound from downstairs he jumped back quickly and in doing so he disrupted the bandana around my eyes and it slipped a little allowing me to see what had really been happening. Obviously, I don't need to tell you what I saw him withdrawing and stuffing back into his pants.

My cousin did not know that for that brief flash I had seen what he was doing and as he removed the blindfold, he told me not to tell anyone about our secret game and off he went downstairs leaving me kneeling in the closet in confusion. As with most of my memories there is just nothingness afterwards.

Third memory: Mud pies. Shortly after the incident at the farm I was playing at making mud pies in the back yard while my mom was picking strawberries. I squatted there on the ground mashing rotten berries and dirt together in a berry basket creating the ultimate strawberry mud pies. As I am laying my mud pies out on a rock to dry in the sun I start telling my mom about the closet and what my cousin had done saying, "I don't think that was very nice cuz boy's pee-pees are nasty cuz that's where they pee from."

I just sat there engrossed in my mud pie venture when I was struck by the silence. I looked up and my mother was just staring at me as if frozen in time, mouth agape. Wordlessly, she came over, picked me up and carried me into the house.

Though I did not hear it I know my mother must have gone to my dad and related to him the tale I had told her. I know in her mind he was her protector and in turn protector to her children. I think she thought that he would not be like his brother and birth father because he had been raised by his aunt and uncle. Wrong on all counts. I don't think she had any clue how far and how deep the roots of depravity ran in that family.

Up until hearing what his brother/cousin had done to me, dad's abuse had only been physical and emotional, but now it was like a whole new world had been opened up for him, it was as if he had been given permission and he now added sexual abuse to the equation. All I know is for me from that point on it was a constant with many painful admonishments as a deterrent to telling mom. As for my brothers I do not know if he crossed that line with them or not and I do not wish to know. It was always harder for me to see them hurt then it was for me to endure it myself, somewhere deep inside me has always hidden a fierce protector.

Forth memory: The bad rocking chair. We had an upholstered rocking chair in our living room that was a little low and open at the sides under the arms. Dad would sit in the rocking chair and ask me to come sit with him, but not in the normal way. I had to sit facing him astraddle, with my legs out to the sides under the arms of the chair so my crotch would be pressed to his. As I sat there he would try to get me to say I hated my mother. He would keep badgering me saying, "what do you think of your mother, you hate her don't you?"

My response was always, "NO. I love her."

Then he would ask "what do you think of me?"

I would always respond with "I don't know."

Instinctively I felt it would be unwise to say I love you as 1: I didn't and 2: that if I said I love you too, it would make me more his in some way and that was terrifying. Pretty mature thinking for a four- year- old child and sad to have been so grown up at such an early age.

Dad trying to get me to say I hated my mother was something he did to me several times the last time I think I was around fifteen and he badgered me with the same litany of questions for almost 2 hours. I remember standing in the archway between the dining and living room as he tried to break me to say I hated her and loved him. I was too afraid of a physical reprisal if I walked away but had the strength of character to stand there and defy him verbally until he tired of it.

Fifth memory: Hot chocolate. Dad had supper and bedtime duties as he worked days and mom waitressed at a local restaurant for the dinner shift. In the cool nights of autumn and winter, dad would make us hot cocoa for our evening snack. I would eagerly drink mine and then feel sick to my stomach and go lay down on the couch. Within short order I would feel the urge to throw up and make a dash for the bathroom. yet he continued to give me the hot cocoa knowing I would get sick.

One unfortunate night I did not make it to the bathroom and puked all over the carpet. Outraged at me for throwing up his good cocoa and making a mess he whipped me with his belt and dragged me through the vomit like a human rag then made me clean up the mess. After that I learned to refuse the hot cocoa. I believe he kept giving me the hot chocolate in anticipation of me throwing up just so he could whip me.

Apparently, I had a mild allergy to cocoa which had gone unnoticed as my mother had not allowed us to have chocolate when we were young. My mom must have heard of my reaction to chocolate minus the brutality and from then on at Easter and Christmas I got white chocolate as that did not make me sick.

Sixth memory: The shaming. My younger brother was a very sweet, loving and emotional child. He was really affected by conflict and sad things. Emotional stress caused him to have trouble going to the bathroom, often only once or twice a week, making potty training extremely difficult. His stools were so big they would get stuck and he would always have smears of poop in his underpants.

One day after cleaning him up dad sent me to get one of my dresses and made me put it on my younger brother. After he was dressed as a girl dad forced my older brother and I to point our fingers at our baby brother and say any hurtful thing we could think of. Considering our age and the era we lived in by today's standards what we said was pretty mild: baby, sissy, stupid. Dad stood behind us smacking our heads and urging us to continue with his usual threats of worse to come if we didn't do as he said.

So, we stood there shaming our baby brother with tears flowing down our faces and for one split second my brother and I locked gazes and we shared a lifetime of hurt in that moment. Each of us saw in the other's eyes the guilt and remorse for what we were doing and the fear and hopelessness of our situation. I believe that at that precise moment was the closest my brother and I had ever been and would ever be.

Seventh memory. Grandmas visit: In the summer of my fifth year my mom's mother came for a visit, it may have been her one and only visit to the brown house, usually we went to visit her at her home. We did not go often to visit my mom's parents but what I can recall of those visits seems pleasant.

Of Italian decent grandma was a little on the short side and very round, her most prominent feature being a tremendous bosom. Grandma was very childlike and collected stuffed monkeys, her favorite she named Bobo. We loved playing with her stuffed monkeys and were also intrigued with the knick-knacks she had displayed on a 3-tiered table in the living room.

Like all our family gatherings the visits were centered around food. (The one thing I was most fortunate of in my childhood is that both sides of the family along with my parents were good cooks.) After dinner grandma would retreat to her little parlor which she kept darkened and cool often with a fan blowing on her. Grandma wore support hose which she always seemed to have rolled down around her ankles making it look like they were rubber tubes. I was fixated by them and had to resist the urge to touch them and ask why they were always rolled down. Too afraid to ask an adult why they did something I kept my thoughts to myself.

The family was gathered on the porch of the brown house enjoying the nice weather. I was sitting on the railing facing my grandmother and she was sitting in a black wicker rocking chair with a flowered cushion on the seat. The chair had long, rather slender rockers with quite a deep curve to them. Talking and laughing, the more animated my grandmother got the faster she rocked until, WHOOSH, it flipped over backwards.

From my vantage point all I could see were those two-rubber tube clad ankles sticking up in the chair. Though she was not hurt she did scream when she fell and of course dad was laughing hysterically his greatest enjoyment derived from someone else's dilemma. Grandma left shortly thereafter and did not visit us again for quite some time even after we moved from that house. I have had a fear of flipping over in a rocking chair ever since and also do not like office chairs that lean back.

CHAPTER 3

The New House

Aside from the memory of my grandmothers visit I really have no other memories from the moment of my brother's shaming until sometime in the winter of age five. That winter mom and dad sold the brown house and we moved in with my grandparents, dads' parents, at the farm.

In the spring, up the road a bit from my grandparents' house in the middle of a cornfield I vaguely remember watching the progress of the foundation being laid for the basement of our new house. I don't remember going to kindergarten except for a brief image of me sitting at a tiny desk wearing a bulky sweater making it winter. I know we were living in our new house when I started first grade but I have only one memory of our stay that winter in my grandparents' home.

First memory: Battle of the nightgown. I am laying, nearly asleep, in the back bedroom of my grandparents' home. I am wearing a long flannel nightgown and my cousin crawls into bed with me. (The same cousin from the closet incident.) He would pull up my nightgown and I would pull it down; this action repeated several times until nothingness takes me away again. Did I lose the battle of the nightgown, most likely? Blissfully retreated into the darkness I have no memory of how far, or if a molestation even occurred. So sad that this is the clearest memory I have of my life for such a long period of time.

After the long winter and spring of darkness, in the summer, I remember being shown which room was to be mine in the new house. There were bunkbeds in the room and I felt excited that they would be mine. There was just that one moment of seeing my room, it was as if I just appeared in the doorway and someone said, "this is your future room."

I don't recall seeing anything else in the house or who it was that showing it to me. My thinking is that being shown my room was just prior to moving in, for I just remembered a snippet of conversation I heard back then that there was some sort of water problem in the basement and we weren't allowed to move in until it was fixed.

Though I do not remember the actual move, I do remember a few things about our early days in the new house, one of which was MUD. Our house had been built in a former cornfield and due to all the excavating, what would eventually become a beautiful green lawn was at that time just a sea of mud.

There was an established road of sorts that ran up the south side of our property that was access to the upper fields. This road was incorporated into our driveway and the only solid ground at that time. Eventually, the driveway would circle up back of the house and down the north side until it again connected to the main road, if seen from above it would look like our hose was sitting in the belly of a giant "D" laying on its side. Dad had created a pathway from the kitchen door out to the solid driveway of raised planks to keep us out of the mud.

Not long after moving into the new house, something wonderful happened, we got a puppy. A big, beautiful fluffy puppy. The only reason I know it was in the early days in our house is I have a memory of carrying the puppy out across the planks to go potty. Technically, I suppose that walking the plank with the puppy is my second memory of that time but it did not come into my mind until quite some years later, whereas the following memory has always stood out clearly.

Second memory: Sea of pee. I awaken on the bottom bunk of my bunkbed, I sit up and swing my legs over to the side, and there sitting next to me on the floor is a pair of red rubber boots. I slip the boots on my bare feet and go out into the hallway and I am immediately greeted by the puppy. Why the boots you ask?

The puppy was confined to the hallway at night as it was linoleum and easy to clean up during potty training and the boots were so I could navigate all the puddles without getting my feet wet. More than likely I carried her out across the planks at that time, but the memory always ends with me standing there in my red rubber boots viewing all the puddles, (and a few mountains.)

I know I am six years old as my birthday is in June and it is summer but recall nothing else of that summer. I remember starting first grade in the fall and the name of my teacher, but nothing of classmates. My early schoolyears are rather hazy and shrouded in sadness and loneliness. I was often ill with bronchitis due to the scarring in my lungs from the chemical pneumonia. I also suffered from chronic kidney infections also attributed to the poisoning, but in retrospect I'm sure were aggravated by the constant sexual abuse.

I was and still am quite knock-kneed which lent itself to me being very uncoordinated. When you add my sickliness, my crooked legs my shyness and the fact I was very withdrawn, let's face it I was an oddity. My differentness made me the last person to be chosen for any team rather in the classroom or the gymnasium.

I have hurtful memories of being the last kid standing among the "undesirables" the poor kids who smelled of bacon grease, kerosene and body odor. Even those kids got chosen before me, as if instinctively my classmates sensed my differentness, my shame, my secret. I cannot place this memory in any particular time as it was a constant throughout my early school years.

Third memory. The matchbook. Up until the time of this memory my memory loss was uncontrollable, it just happened, and awareness would just pop in or out.

Dad, called me into my parent's bedroom and made me lie down on my mother's side of the bed and pull my pants down. As he started touching me I picked up a book of matches from the nightstand and focused on the letters and not what was happening to me. I felt myself drawn into the lettering and I was gone; only coming back into myself and into reality when I felt dad leave the bed and go into the bathroom.

I stand up, pull up my pants and leave the room. I do not think the abuse was daily, but it was frequent, and after that one time of using the matchbook to disappear, I no longer needed it, all I had to do was picture the matchbook in my mind and I was gone.

The thing that makes me so sad and angry about this memory is that by that tender age the abuse had already become routine. I see the hopelessness written on my face as I enter the room, yes, I said see. In my most painful memories it is as if I am floating above my body and witnessing my own degradation, I see everything leading up to the actual molestation when I leave, down to the expression on my face.

Forth memory: Normal childhood. Not a single memory but rather a collection of typical childhood activities, that because of their repetition, can be placed in no specific time or order but occurred in between the blank spaces.

Birthday presents were not common, instead we got to choose our favorite meal. I usually picked ham or lasagna. After our birthday meal we would always go down to my grandparents' house for homemade, hand cranked ice-cream and cake, the birthday celebrant got to lick the beater.

I remember playing with the neighbor kids who matched my brothers and I in age. Climbing trees, riding bike, fishing, arguing with my brothers, long walks, collecting wildflowers, picking berries, sleigh riding and ice skating. I experienced real joy in these childhood pursuits, somehow, I was able to step out of the shadow of my secret life.

Fifth memory: An ugly dog. My parents had subscribed to a magazine about pedigreed dogs after getting our puppy. The magazine showed pictures of many exotic breeds one of which is a Chinese Crested dog. It is a small, thin bodied dog whose most outstanding characteristic is random splotches of hair sticking out all over its mostly bare skin. In a word homely.

Dad had cut a picture of one of these dogs out of an issue and kept it in a drawer in the china hutch and would periodically take it out and put in front of my face and tell me I was as ugly as this dog. For further insult, at some point, someone had acquired a fake pile of dog poop made of plaster and colored a nasty orange-brown. Dad would place the fake poop on my dinner plate alongside the picture of the dog and tell me that's all I deserved to eat because I was so ugly and worthless.

Of course, it would be put away as soon as mom's car was heard pulling in the driveway.

When I retreated from an abusive situation, I always came back as a new me that was able to find happiness in simple childhood things. I still had memory of the bad things, I felt sadness and fear but not to the extent that I was debilitated by them. Somehow, I was able to come back strong enough, not to just survive until the next abuse but enjoy life in between the abuses. Looking back, I can see that it was an amazing ability.

Often throughout my life I have heard of or known people that had endured similar abuses as mine and they were completely incapable of ever getting past "the bad stuff" to experience any joy. You may wonder how, after reading my tale so far, that I am able to make this next statement: "I must have been blessed."

CHAPTER 4

The Lessons and Games Begin

First memory: Second grade: Only two things stand out about that year and they are intertwined, the foremost being that I discovered the joy of reading. Once I had mastered reading I became a book addict, it was another avenue of escape for me from the reality of my life. It was more enjoyable to journey along with the characters in the stories I was reading. I can remember ALWAYS reading, I would get annoyed if I had to leave my book, literally, as I completely immersed myself into whatever story I was reading.

I even read at recess while the other students were playing around me. My usual spot was sitting on the curb in front of the school where the buses picked us up and dropped us off, my back against a pillar in an attempt to hide myself, so I could enjoy my trip into storyland.

One particular day, engrossed in my book, I did not hear the bell ending recess nor notice the students filing past me back into the school. I don't remember what it was that precipitated my coming back to reality, one second, I'm sitting there and the next image that pops into my mind is me running in the door, through the lobby, around the corner to the right and crashing smack dab into another girl coming the opposite direction. Our foreheads smacked together like a bowling ball hitting the pins and down we both went, on our butts, matching goose eggs already appearing on our respective foreheads. We laughed, introduced ourselves, and became best friends.

I don't remember her being in my classroom as I believe there were two teachers for each grade at that time. We talked at recess I'm sure but can't remember doing so, though I do remember having sleepovers at her house a few times, always her house, not mine. We remained friends until seventh grade when her family moved away. She was the first friend I ever made.

Second memory: Laundry lesson. Dad could never just show or teach my brothers and I anything without it becoming a lesson in pain too. Every lesson was accompanied by a punch, a kick, or a smack with the handle of something along with a verbal berating of how stupid and worthless we were.

One day dad, called me into the bathroom and told me to sort the laundry for washing. He stood there silently watching until I had removed everything from the hamper and placed them in piles, he then yelled at me to sit on the edge of the tub. Dad scooped all the laundry into one pile and commenced to give me my real lesson in proper laundry sorting.

I sat there, on the edge of the tub, trembling in fear with tears running down my face as he yelled out, "darks don't go with colors and whites are always separate!"

Dad then proceeded to sort the laundry and as he picked up each piece and put it into its properly color-coded pile he took his fist and punched one of my knees, alternating knees every time he placed a piece of laundry in its correct pile.

"This goes in this pile, BOOM and this goes in this pile BOOM."

Every last piece etched in my mind by painful example until all the laundry was sorted.

When the lesson was over I had to pick up a load of laundry and carry it out to the kitchen where the washing machine was. I could not openly sob for I knew doing so would encourage more beating. So, hiccoughing and gulping air in a futile attempt not to cry I started limping down the hall on my swollen, mushy knees with the load of laundry in my arms, dad behind me kicking me and telling me to, "stop crying or I'll give you something to cry about."

Laundry started I was told to go put long pants on so mom would not see my knees and given the lie to tell her about why I was limping.

I knew the consequences and from then on, I was very diligent in my laundry sorting duties.

Third memory: Chicken pox. I contracted chicken pox sometime between the ages of seven and eight. I had a particularly severe case the pox even in my eyes. The doctor told my mother to have me wear sun glasses to help protect my eyes and that the sun glasses would also help alleviate some of the pain the sun caused them. Not having a pair of her own mom borrowed a pair from my grandmother, they were thick framed and very dark. To my misfortune I was wearing them on a laundry day.

Dad had carried a load of laundry out to the kitchen and set it on the floor in preparation of starting a load. Disastrous timing had me coming in from outside wearing the dark glasses at that precise moment. Before my eyes could adjust to the dim interior lighting or remove the sunglasses, dad yelled at me to hand him a striped towel from the pile. The towel he asked for had red, blue and yellow stripes, in my near blindness I reached down and grabbed at a towel with those same colors but by mistake grabbed another which also had red, blue and yellow, only they were polka-dots. I immediately realized my error, but it was too late.

Dad was across the room in a flash and had me by the back of the neck and forced me to my knees and commenced to smash my face repeatedly into the pile of dirty clothes screaming at the top of his voice, "this is a stripe!"

The really sad part is that both towels went into the same load and his reaction unnecessary. As for my grandmothers' sun glasses, I was made to tell her that I was running, tripped and fell on them. Sadder still, I was never able to run, either my lungs gave out or my knocked knees.

Fourth memory: Let the games begin. After moving into our new house, dad invented new "games" for us, as watching us get zapped by static electricity just didn't do it for him anymore.

My brothers and I were sent to the kitchen to get pieces of plastic wrap and then instructed to hold the plastic wrap tautly across our mouths and suck in while twisting it to form a bubble. We then had to bite the bubbles to explode them, which stung our tongues. It was not just once we had to keep doing it until every square inch of plastic wrap had been used with him watching and laughing each time we winced.

We tried to get small pieces so we wouldn't have to do too many bubbles but with a swift kick in the ass he would send us back to the kitchen for a larger piece. As you have probably noticed ass kicking was one of his go to cruelties, ranging from mild to airborne.

Fifth memory: Game two. Another of dads' fun things to do was for him to lick the palm of his hand and taking us by the wrist so we couldn't pull away, he would rub his wet palm in a circle on our forearms so that our arm hair would form into knots. When he had made 5 or 6 knots he would pluck them off.

The knot game and the bubble game were often "played" back to back. Not allowed to flinch or cry and if asked if it was fun, we knew we had to say yes. Never content to just do it himself we had to do it to ourselves and each other.

There are a few other games that I will present here even though they did not necessarily begin in this time period, but to show the progression of cruelty. Frankly it is hard for me to place much of this on a time line, once a game started it was continuous throughout our youth.

We had to learn to stand on our heads and until it was mastered there was much yelling and hitting but once mastered he didn't ask us to do it for his pleasure was in the torture of teaching us. If there was no pain involved it no longer interested him.

The suffocation game is one he started in our teen years (he probably had to wait for us to get taller for this to work) dad would stand behind one of us and wrap his arms around our chests, he would then instruct us to take a very deep breath and then exhale with all the force we had while he squeezed us with his arms so tightly, that we would pass out from lack of oxygen. We were also made to do this to each other multiple times until we too could achieve our sibling fainting.

Dad was like a mad scientist and was always making some kind of gadget out of a shoebox or whatnot. They had glowing lights and made various sounds and were powered by batteries. There was always some contraption setting on a little black desk in our dining room, the drawer in the desk had spare batteries for his little projects.

One day my older brother, came in from doing some sweaty outside work and for reasons known only to dad had my brother stand there while he took a good size battery from the drawer and put it to his sweaty forehead. Dad, on another occasion put a battery on my sweaty arm too.

Throughout my life I read and heard about cases of child abuse and the common misconception that prevailed for years is that it only occurred in poor families or was a result of alcoholism.

We were not poor, granted at times my parents had to juggle finances, we were middle class in the area I grew up in. Dad drank upon occasion but it was not to be problem drinking until we were grown and then for the most part only a payday binge night.

My parents were educated and far from ignorant. Dad by the standards of the time could have been classified as brilliant. Higher learning was always encouraged and my brothers and I were included in intelligent conversation. The house was filled with books and magazines ranging through classics, science, metaphysics and we all read them. Our house was clean, we were well fed, had nice clothes, we did not want for anything.

Holidays were a big deal and much planning went into to them especially Christmas. Dad would shop alone and with mom to find us each the perfect gifts to suit our personalities.

We all got caught up in the spirit of giving even in selecting a present for dad. Odd as it may seem we often felt a desperate kind of love for him or maybe it was just a hope that if we did something or gave something nice it would somehow make it all better.

Dad had a keen wit and he could always make us laugh, there were joyful family times, but you never knew when the change would occur. Looking back, I do believe he was a split personality, the happy, fun loving, Dr. Jekyll one minute and the evil Mr. Hyde the next.

The abuse aside it was often very hard as a child to reconcile the disparate emotions in my mind. How could I love and respect him as I was taught to do and still hate and fear him at the same time?

I just decided it was a flaw in me. There were times and things I truly loved about him. I felt guilt and a sense of betrayal to myself for loving him and guilt for hating him. This pattern of feeling guilty for everything has been a constant struggle for me my whole life. Even at the age of 57 it still raises its ugly head, it most definitely is one of the hardest mindsets to overcome when you have been a victim of emotional abuse over an extended period of time.

Do not lose heart, abuse can be overcome. The first and biggest step is acknowledging it. You have to own it, take it into your being so that you can express all the emotions attached to it. Once acknowledged you can then start the process of releasing all that crap. I know how hard it is to overcome the victim mindset of worthlessness.

At times it is easier to think of yourself in a negative context because it is familiar, even comfortable, having been a part of your life for so long. I still do it to myself, even in the writing of this book when faced with the challenge of figuring out how to use my computer, in my frustration, the trained parrot in my head started its litany of you're stupid, worthless. I had to pluck his feathers and get past it, I am still getting past it.

Sixth memory: Punishment. Punishment was a constant throughout my childhood like the other abuses and a ritualistic spin was put on it to maximize the fear and dread. Whenever one of us kids had done something to deserve a spanking, it became a psychological punishment too. Dad called his belt, "the black snake."

The belt was kept on a hook in my parents' bathroom. We would be sent to get it so we had to hand/offer it to dad for our whipping. The hallway seemed a mile long and we tried to walk slowly to stall off the inevitable, but soon learned we got extra lashes if we took too long. Upon occasion dad would walk behind us smacking and threatening us in both directions. Even when he followed us to retrieve the belt we still had to carry it back to the living room and present it to him.

Whippings were done in the living room with plenty of room to swing and with an audience. Other times we would be sent next door to the neighbors' yard to cut a switch from the lilac bush and it better be a good one or you were sent back for another and lashes added. Both instruments of pain caused welts and bruises. Sometimes, all three of us would get spanked one after the other his thinking we were all in on whatever misdeed.

Dad would yell at my brothers and I in front of mom and administer some mild spanking (as if any spanking is mild) but not kick or punch us. Mom knew about his temper but I don't think she knew or more likely feared to acknowledge his ultra-cruel side. Did mom suspect the brutality? Either way, she knew enough to tell us to stop something or get something done before dad got home.

Knowing how the mind of a victim works first hand, I believe she felt powerless. As I finished recounting this last paragraph I had a memory pop in of an incident that happened while we were still living in the brown house.

Seventh memory: Aimless. Mom had bundled my brothers and I into the backseat of the car and just aimlessly drove us around. Mom was sobbing and talking out loud and kept repeating, "I don't know what to do, I don't know where to go, I have no one." Witnessing moms' distress my brothers and I started crying too. To calm us she gave each of us a coconut bon-bon from an open bag on the front seat, saying she didn't have anything else for us and no money. Mom drove around for quite some time until we had all calmed down and then she turned back home.

In my adult mind's eye, I see myself then, watching her face reflected in the rearview mirror. I can now see and recognize the look of resignation and defeat in her posture and face on that day. I guess I just answered my own question, she felt powerless.

My mother had her own family dynamics to deal with, which at some point she had confided to me. Mom was the eldest of four siblings and the least favorite of her mother. In fact, her mother pretty much hated her.

My grandmother became pregnant out of wedlock and was forced to marry my grandfather who was quite a bit older than her. The circumstances of that situation I do not know, rape or innocent exploration gone wrong, either way it is lost to history now? The sad result of that forced marriage is that my grandmother was wed to a man she did not love and blamed my mothers' existence for it.

Considering some of the things my grandmother did to my mother when she was growing up I'm leaning towards the rape theory. My grandmother's animosity towards my mother did not extend to her other children, she doted on my aunt and uncles. My grandfather's feelings were exactly the opposite, he adored my mother for her conception landed him his prize, my grandmother. My mother also told me she had been raped by an uncle and had been targeted by a female cousin that was a lesbian who wanted her to become a lesbian too.

From the beginning there was discord between my grandmother and my mother over her choice of husbands. My mother told me that in defiance of her mother she dated and then married my father to pretty much piss her mother off as grandma did not like my father or his parents. When my mother subsequently divorced my father and married his brother it did not endear her any closer to her mother who clung to the adage, "you made your own bed, now lie in it."

In time, after all her children were grown and settled my grandmother finally divorced my grandfather and eventually remarried. In her new-found happiness she seemed to accept my mother a little more and visits became more frequent. On the other hand, my grandfather never got over grandma leaving him and mourned her until the day he died.

CHAPTER 5

Rules to Live By

The first few years of living in our new house my parents both worked days. Mom worked at a grocery store and her hours extended into the evenings a bit during the week and until 8 or 9 on Friday nights. Working in a factory dad was the parent who got home first and had the responsibility of cooking dinner.

I know it was dad that taught my older brother and I how to cook and I am sure there were multiple lessons but I can only recall one image of my brother and I standing on a chair in front of the stove tending to something on the burner. I'm certain our mutual cooking lessons from dad were as cruel and full of violence as everything else he taught us and most likely why I cannot remember them. Mom often worked Saturday mornings as well which left one or both of us to prepare dads' breakfast. I have a very BOLD memory of a solo cooking lesson with dad.

First memory: Follow the procedure. No task, no matter how small, was without dads' stamp of cruelty. In this memory Dad was grilling me, (pun intended) on the proper procedure to preparing his breakfast. It was not just how to cook the meal I had to recite, but every step from getting pans out of the cupboard, food out of refrigerator, silverware out of drawer to serving the meal.

I remember going through the steps of pulling pans out of cupboard, cracking eggs to serving only to be told it was wrong and getting smacked upside the head and made to repeat it again, until in his frustration at my stupidity (his word) dad told me the proper sequence, using his fist as punctuation.

Even though I had recited the proper way to prepare each item I had not done it in the correct order for their individual cook times. I had been, in my recitation starting the eggs before I started the coffee, which took the longest. My head hurt so much from all those whacks and my arm from the punches that I can still recite the proper breakfast procedure to this day.

1: Get coffee pot out of cupboard, fill with water, place filter in basket, add four scoops of coffee, replace lid, set on back right burner, set heat at medium high.

2: Take frying pan out of cupboard and place on right front burner, get turner out of drawer, take eggs and butter out of refrigerator and place on counter, get bread out of bread box and take two slices and place in toaster (DO NOT PUT DOWN) place slice of butter in frying pan. Take silverware out of drawer and place on table, set plate next to stove.

3: Watch for coffee to come to a boil then turn burner to medium low so it only perks and doesn't boil over, set timer for coffee at 7 minutes.

4: When coffee timer shows 4 minutes left turn front burner on medium wait for butter to melt and crack 2 eggs into frying pan (praying the yolks don't break) as soon as the egg whites start to set put down toast and gently flip eggs and turn off stove as it is an electric stove and burner stays hot and you do not want the eggs to get too done.

5: Toast pops up, butter toast, serve up eggs. Turn off timer which is dinging, turn off coffee and remove from burner so grounds settle.

6: Place plate of food in front of dad, go back and pour coffee, add some milk not too much just to the right shade of brown, serve coffee…. the end.

I know that I cooked every day meals with my mom too but just can't seem to remember doing it. I do however remember helping her with Sunday dinners after church. We always used a tablecloth on

Sunday and I got to choose which one, a favorite of mine had red geraniums on it.

I have many happy visions in my head of helping mom with the holiday meals and baking. We always prepared an insane amount of food and goodies for the holidays. Mom and I made hundreds of cookies, multiple loaves of different sweet breads and pies. There were ginormous turkeys to stuff, hams to glaze and goose to baste. Our house was the gathering place for the extended family and for the most part very happy at holiday times.

I also enjoyed gardening with my mom and even pulling weeds as long as dad wasn't around for he could suck the joy out of any project and instill fear just by his mere presence. My mom and I would pick berries all summer, and harvest load after load of produce from our huge garden. I would help her can tomatoes, pickles, relishes and other vegetables, along with a variety of jams and jellies.

I loved doing all these things and still do. There were some chores though, under the supervision of dad, which are recalled in painful memory.

Second memory: Trees. Our property was mostly treeless except for a few stragglers on the side hill due to its having been a field. Dad bought a slew of pine seedling trees to plant around the house as windbreak and on the hill to help prevent erosion.

Dad had laid out a line of holes for the baby trees and it was the job of my brother and me to hold the trees perfectly straight in their individual holes while dad filled the dirt back in around them.

You can probably guess that not too many trees were straight and there were multiple knocks in the head with the shovel handle and numerous kicks in the ass that threw us forward so our faces smashed into the ground as we had to kneel to hold the trees. I received the worst kick of my life while planting those trees sending me sailing through the air nearly 5 feet. I think helping to plant those trees is one of the root causes of the back and knee problems I have suffered from most of my life.

Third memory: Third grade. I recall sitting at my desk and just burning up with fever, I was so hot and my lower back ached. I don't know if I passed out or fell asleep but the next thing I know I am being picked up by my teacher and carried to the nurses' office where they took my temperature finding it to be 103, they immediately called my mother.

Mom came and took me to the doctors' office where I was diagnosed with a severe kidney infection. In fact, I missed so many days that year I nearly did not advance to the next grade. I also missed many of my Brownie meetings due to illness and they almost didn't give me my wings to fly up to the next level which was Girl Scouts.

That school year I actually remember my teachers' name and what she looked like. Grey haired and plump, she was very grandmotherly, truly loved by all her students. My brothers also had her for third grade and the crafts we each made in her class became staples in our holiday decorating until they had crumbled to dust.

Fourth memory: Another rocking chair. The whole family had gone down to my grandparents' house to watch one of the Apollo rocket missions on television as they had a bigger TV set. My grandmother had an antique glider rocking chair in the living room and because of its age and daintiness we kids were not allowed to sit in it.

Me and my brothers assumed our customary positions on the living room floor, chin in hands, to watch the footage on TV. Engrossed in what I was watching my foot wandered over and started tapping the rocker and making it move, Dad yelled at me to stop moving the chair and preceded to tell me that it was bad luck to rock a chair with no one in it or someone would die.

Chastised, I moved my foot, but once again, unconsciously, my foot wandered back and again began tapping the chair. Next thing I knew I was being snatched up from the floor by my hair and was shaken like a rag doll and beaten until when let go I just collapsed into a pile on the floor. I retreated to never, never land and did not have any awareness for several months.

My great-grandmother lived with my grandparents at the farm or I should say they lived with her as it was her husband's farm, my great-grandfathers, whom I had never met as he died long before I was born.

I have a few memories of my great-grandmother, one being she would pay me ten cents to water the houseplants for her. She would give my brothers and I horehound candies, which we hated. We would hold the candies between our teeth and try to say, "thank you grandma" without the candy touching our tongue. We would run outside and spit them out listening to great-grandma chuckling in the background for she knew we didn't like them.

The day I got beat for rocking the chair, (unknown to me the full circumstances to her being bedridden at that time) my great-grandma was lying in the next room dying of cancer.

My next recollection that year, some months after the rocking chair incident, was of my mom getting an urgent call from my grandmother to come quickly and she leaves. I struggle into my snowsuit and start running down the road to my grandparents' house, I see myself about halfway there and then nothingness again.

Technically I suppose, this is two separate memories but they are entwined and come out together. Me a crumpled pile on the floor of my grandparents' living room floor and then flash forwarded to me trotting down the road in my red snowsuit.

What I learned later is that my great-grandma died that winter day of bone cancer and I was sure that I had been the cause of her ultimate death by rocking the empty rocking chair earlier that summer. I believed this and carried the guilt of this for many years.

To this day if I enter a room and bump a rocking chair and it moves, or if someone gets up from a rocking chair and it is still moving, I instinctively reach out my hand to stop it. I rarely have owned a rocking chair still feeling uncomfortable around them.

Fifth memory: The groping. In the waning light of autumn and winter, dad created a new game just for me. Dad shut the lights off and had us all crawl around on our hands and knees on the floor and dad would reach out from the darkness behind a chair or under the table to grab us.

My brothers would squeal and scurry away thinking he was in pursuit when in reality he was waiting for me. Grabbing me from under the table he held on tightly and start groping me. My brothers unaware of the game change, giggling in the distance involved in their own version of the game.

Dad begged and pleaded with me not to struggle. I remember his voice took on a creepy childlike quality as he begged me to stay. The tone he used scared me more than if he threatened me like he usually did, The NEED in his voice made my skin crawl. The desperation in his voice had the sound of tears ready to fall. I can still hear it.

"Please, please, please, don't go, let me touch you."

All these years later and I'm still repulsed. When I finally break free the whining child is gone and the mean pissed off father is back in control, the lights go on and the ass kicking resumes, yelling at me and my brothers to get the chores done before mom gets home.

I remember afterwards following my brother down the hall with a mop as he is vacuuming in front of me, dad kicking my ass, urging us to get done faster because supper needs to be fixed too.

Somewhere in this time frame I developed the ability to see auras around people. I asked my mother what they were and she explained and gave me a book to read that talked about them. I wondered why dads was sometimes blue and other times brown.

I also saw auras or energy fields around houses and buildings. Mom was very interested in metaphysics and our house was filled with books on alternative subjects, I openly asked her questions on some of the subjects and we had good conversations.

Eventually, I quit seeing auras and instead perceived energy from people and places. The energy I felt was accompanied by a warm glow and an involuntary smile if the energy was positive. If it felt negative to me I got gooseflesh pimples and a sense of drawing in on myself. I would read people we passed while riding in the car and whom I met on the street when in town. It became a secret game to me that I never told anyone about until now.

What would dad have done if he had found out that I could sense when the "monster" was taking over.

Sixth memory: Urge to kill. I am not sure exactly when this abuse started but it was frequent enough and horrific enough to create a blood lust in me.

Dad would lie on the sofa on his left side and make me stretch out next to him and he would cover us both with an afghan. He would hold my left wrist in his left hand and bend it back whispering to me that he would snap my wrist if I made a sound to alert my brothers who were laying on the floor in front of us watching TV.

Holding me physically and mentally captive he would then proceed to molest me with his other hand all the time threatening to hurt me or my brothers or even kill them describing in detail, just how, in a whisper, with his lips to my ear so only I could hear. This debauchery with my brothers present ignited a flame of hatred so strong in me that I wanted to kill him.

When dad got home from work or on weekends he would often lie on the couch on his back and take a nap, his snores loud and steady. Each snore a thrum of hatred in my veins. I remember on several occasions tip toeing into the kitchen and ever so slowly (it was the only drawer that squealed when opened) opening the kitchen drawer that held the knives and selecting a large long bladed knife.

Taking the knife, I would then cautiously creep into the living room and stand with the knife raised over the vicinity of his heart. A film of the cruel, evil, disgusting things he had done to me running through my mind accompanied by a sound track repeating "I hate you" like a broken record repeating the same thing.

I stand, shaking in pent up anger and hatred, tears streaming down my face, poised to make the plunge. Obviously, I never did stab him, but it was not fear of killing that stayed my hand but the fear that I wouldn't do it right and only glance off a rib. I was so afraid of missing my target and dad stabbing me instead.

All the years of dads' self- esteem busting rhetoric, "you're stupid, you can't do anything right" was running through my mind at the same time as my broken record of "I hate you." The strong me and the weak me canceling each other out, stayed my hand.

I simply did not think I could hit the right spot. I would lower the knife and creep back into the kitchen and put it away. I repeated this act several times with the same outcome. I often questioned myself over the years on why I didn't just cut his throat? I was always only focused on cutting out his black heart.

One summer we got a new babysitter. The neighbor girl who had been our sitter was killed in an automobile accident. The new sitter mom had met through her job at the grocery store. I remember the new sitter was funny, upbeat, a real child of the sixties and I liked her. We would dance, sing and she would do my hair. Here was a stranger that liked me, showed real interest in me and I was completely at ease in her company.

Seventh memory: The telling. I can see it so clearly, I am helping her clean up after lunch, she is washing dishes and I am putting stuff away in the refrigerator. I start telling her about dad and asked her if her dad touches her the same way too. It was very conversational, I wasn't upset, just matter of fact.

The perverse and unnatural things that were being done to me had been part of my daily life for so long that I had become mostly emotionless to them. In fact, I did not show or feel emotions and felt like a freak. I would pretend emotions so no one would notice me not reacting, my mind analyzing those around me so I would show the fake proper emotion. I had built a protective shell around my emotions which enabled me to keep going through the motions.

Looking up, after closing the refrigerator door, the babysitter is looking at me in horror and becomes hysterical, crying, hugging me and rattling on about how horrible it was, how un-natural and Oh my God, you might get pregnant!

Naturally, I too became hysterical and started sobbing as I was sure that I had done something wrong and even more sure that dad was going to kill me. I do not know where my brothers were during all this, I have no recollection of them at all. The sitter called my mom at work to tell her she had something urgent to talk to her about and then she put me in her car to drive me to moms' work.

From the moment I get in the car I have no memory until later that night. Laying in my bed (I now have a big antique four post bed) I hear my parents arguing out in the living room. I heard mom ask dad about what the babysitter had told her and I heard him respond that it was all a lie made up by the babysitter and me, then nothingness until I awoke to my mom getting into bed with me.

My mother slept with me for about 3 weeks before going back to my dads' bed. The molestations resumed shortly thereafter and being a fatalist at the ripe old age of 9 I did not tell mom, figuring it didn't work the first time why bother. I just became craftier at avoiding dad and mom took some measures that no more "misunderstandings" would occur by arranging for me to stay at her friends' house after school and I rode home with my mom when she got out of work.

I felt grateful about not being home with dad, but I did feel guilty about abandoning my brothers. I asked my bubble people to protect them. My brothers never confided in me if dad took out revenge on them over my escape, the stricture of "don't tell or else" had been beat into us. Dad was big on retribution, so I'm reasonably sure they took some form of punishment for my deliverance.

CHAPTER 6

Womanhood and Wisdom

After the telling, the frequency of my sexual abuse lessened as I was not at home most of the time and I learned to be very evasive when I was home. While dad was distracted or busy I would sneak away, fishing or hiking. I also enlisted the help of my brothers and confided in them what had been happening.

For some reason my older brother did not believe me, I don't know why, maybe it was too much of a burden for him to take on with all the fears he already had to cope with. My younger brother did believe me, gentle soul that he was, would come to me if he was going to leave the house to warn me so I would not be left alone with dad, enabling me to make my escape too.

It was around this time that I began having major déjà vu. I would have déjà vu multiple times a day not just one random happening. Often it would happen with every conversation I was included in for a whole day. Like I did when I got the vibrational feelings about people I made a sort of game out of my déjà vu experiences too, another secret all to myself.

When I would enter into a conversation with someone and remember having had it already. I would, one time, repeat it verbatim to see if the outcome of my conversation would be the same as in the "dream." At other times I would say to myself "ok, I said it this way when I dreamed it, now I'll say these words instead and see what the outcome will be."

In doing this I was able to avoid some of the petty little arguments that kids have. I did not always avoid the arguments as I continually challenged myself by not changing words to see if it would still follow true.

Along with the déjà vu came the ability to council. If someone asked me for advice or information about something, even if I knew nothing about the subject, I was able to answer accurately. I would feel a larger presence well up inside me and answer the question. My human self was so timid and my self-esteem nearly non-existent that afterwards I would search books or ask an adult about the subject, to see if what had come out of my mouth was true. It always was. I did not let it swell my head even at a young age I was cautious about EGO though I did not even know what it was at that time.

First memory: Womanhood. In the summer of my tenth year, (as if I didn't feel enough of a freak) just before school started in August, I went to bed one night and awoke the next day with breasts. It literally was overnight from flat to "B" cup no training bra just HELLO, instant hooters.

My newly sprouted breasts not only garnered me more ogling from dad who would now just stare at my chest whenever he talked to me but when school started my class mates would dare me to prove they were real. I remember being followed into the restroom at school where some girls cornered me and made me lift my shirt to prove they were real and not tissues stuffed in my bra.

It wasn't long before I got my next dose of womanhood. The appearance of my breasts a precursor to when Mother Nature, blessed me with my first menstrual cycle.

We always got on the school bus from our neighbor's house, (as it was closer to the road) when halfway across the yard to their house one day, I got sick to my stomach and threw up. Turning around I yacked my way back home and discovered the cause of my sudden illness.

What makes this memory doubly stand out is that I had eaten an English muffin for breakfast and when it came up it came out my nose. My sinuses and nose were completely packed with undigested English muffin and it burned like the devil. It took me nearly all day to get it blown out of my sinuses.

Two things came out of this incident, one being a curiosity about the human body for I was totally amazed that you could vomit out your nose. Secondly my period gave me a huge advantage over my sexual abuse, though the abuse had slowed it still happened at times.

I happened to recall, after my period started, a conversation I had overheard between my mom and one of her friends in which my mom had told her friend that dad had an absolute aversion to women when they were on their periods to the point that he did not even like to sleep in the same bed as my mother let alone have any sexual intimacy when she had her period.

My brilliant solution was to soak a sanitary napkin with fake blood I made with food coloring and hide it in my closet. When times came up that I would be home without mom I would put the fake napkin on and complain of cramps.

Second memory: A friend for me. When I was eleven we switched churches because the minister of our previous church had freaked out on my mother when she had tried to talk to him about some of her spiritual beliefs.

In our switch to the new church I became friends with a girl in Sunday school, a distant neighbor who rode on my bus, but being a couple of years older than me we had not been friends in school. In the country two miles away is still considered a neighbor. We became best friends from that time on and I spent many nights at her house.

Delia's house was quite old, very nicely kept and extremely haunted. Throughout the history of the house there were records of several people having died in the house one of which was a suicide. This tortured soul floated about the house in a brown/grey mist sobbing.

The other ghosts would all try and talk to me at the same time until I learned to block them out. I was only able to see the suicide ghost, but I could hear all the other ghosts. I wasn't really scared of them just annoyed for they kept me awake all night and staying with my friend was my refuge.

When I was there I didn't have to worry about dad. My friend and I shared our personal miseries, for while I had the evil stepfather, she had the evil adoptive mother, we were each other's sounding board and strength. We remain friends to this day.

Third memory: UFO. It was a nice summer day and I had ridden my bike down to the farm below my grandparent's house, owned by the family of the babysitter who had died in the car accident. There were two more girls in the family one several years older than me and one two years younger than me. I was helping the elder of the two to round up some stray cows.

We rode our bikes down the road to where there was a break in the fence and some cows were out. Leaving our bikes at the side of the road we walked down into the field to herd the cows back up that had gotten out through the broken fence.

Moving the cows along we glanced up and saw something unusual on the road a little way beyond where we had left our bikes. Herding the cows through the gap we hurriedly fixed the fence and started back up across the field. Our minds not comprehending what we saw in those first moments because we both said, "it must be some more cows out."

Walking up to our bikes we mounted them and started peddling towards the object on the road. What finally registered to our minds and sight was a large silver dome shaped object that encompassed the full width of the road. Mesmerized, we peddled faster, and it started moving away from us until WHOOSH it just shot up into the sky almost faster than you can blink.

Backtracking to where it had been sitting on the road I noticed that all the stones were burnt black in a ring. At that point the other girl became scared and took off lickity-split for her house. Me, I was just plain old excited. I hopped on my bike and rode home as fast as I could to get my mother. Mom drove the car to where I had seen the UFO and we both examined the stones, (it was a dirt road) and felt the tingling energy that was left behind.

The neighbor girl would never speak of it again and as for me I became a UFO addict. From that day forward, I would spend many hours watching the sky day and night for further sightings.

My brothers and I along with the neighbor kids spent hours outside playing and we all watched for mysteries in the sky. From the time I saw the UFO on the road in 1971 we witnessed many unusual sightings.

We lived in the country in the bend of a river and a common

sight for us kids for several summers was watching glowing orbs that would descend and drop behind the tree line and look as if they were going into the river, some nights we counted as many as 30. As I read more about UFOs a common theme emerged of sightings being most prevalent in rural areas and near bodies of water, we had both.

Fourth memory: Road to nowhere. Although, chronologically, this memory is out of sequence, it popped in my head after writing about the UFO. Might they be related? The road I'm about to write about starts at the farm where I followed the UFO where it is part of a four-way intersection.

There were two roads that could be taken into where we lived, the main road mostly paved except for the last quarter mile on dirt road, and the mountain road. The mountain road (as we called it then) was a single lane dirt road (with only a few spaces wide enough for two cars to pass) that hugged the backside of the mountain behind our house and followed the curve of the river which could be seen through the trees below. The road was approximately two miles long and intersected the paved main road on the other end.

My brothers and I along with the neighbor kids all road our bikes out there enjoying the shaded, woodsy, peacefulness. The only thing that marred its beauty was about half-way out, over the years, people had dumped trash. We used the dump as a mile marker to gauge how far we had gone.

When I was fifteen or sixteen years old one of the neighbor girls and I rode our bikes out the mountain road and down into a little village to get a popsicle. (yes, in those days we would ride bike three miles for a nickel popsicle.) Eating our popsicles, we headed back towards home on the mountain road.

The next thing you know we were coming out into the sun on the opposite end of the road. We looked at each other and asked each other at the same time, "do you remember passing the dump?"

Neither of us remembered passing the dump and spooked and confused we pedaled quickly for home. Upon returning home and checking the clock we were even more spooked to learn that we had lost time.

This was a common trip for us and we knew that on our bikes it was less than 2 hours there and back and that day it was four hours. Where had we been for two hours? We never rode our bikes out the mountain road again.

Through conversations over the years I learned that other people had lost time out there too with no one having any recollection. In later years I drove out the road in a car with no adverse effects.

Not sure if it was the proximity of the river and the land creating some kind of portal. But some 5 miles from the mountain road on the main, paved, state route, running along the rivers' path there was an area where several people I knew had lost time too.

There are numerous mysterious energy spots all over the world, many well documented. One of the most famous, the Bermuda triangle. In these certain spots people have lost minutes, hours, days and sometime disappearing altogether.

CHAPTER 7

❖

One Last time

My mother had very bad knees, a genetic disorder that ran in her family, causing her much pain. In the summer of 1972 the doctors finally decided to do something about it and scheduled surgery for my mother to have a knee replacement.

A few days before mom left for the hospital she took me to stay with relatives a wife of one of dad's cousins whom mom was friends with and a fellow psychic. My mother and I visited her enough that I referred to her as aunt. It was planned that I was to travel with her to visit her family and stay with her for the duration of mom's hospital stay so I wouldn't be home with dad without mom there.

In those days this type of surgery was fairly new and stay times in the hospital were much longer than they are today, and mom's hospitalization was expected to be a week. It was raining when mom checked into the hospital the day before surgery and raining when I left on my trip with my aunt. The storm generated one of the worst floods to ever be recorded and took its place in history.

First memory: Porn and gin. Because of all the flooding my "aunt" cut our visit short in and we came back home. After we got home we learned of all the flood damage and found out that my mother was stranded in the hospital completely cut off by high water and washed out bridges. Dad seizing the opportunity, ridge running over mountain tops out of the flood waters he came and took me home over the protests of my "aunt."

Walking into the living room after over a week of being away I spotted sitting on the floor a box of books, curious, as I loved books, I picked one up only to discover that it was pornography as were all the rest, embarrassed I dropped it looking to see if anyone had noticed.

That night after my brothers had gone to bed dad called me out to the living room and gave me a drink, it was a gin gimlet, very nasty tasting but I was forced to drink it and others so that I was drunk and unable to fend off his assault on me. I don't remember anything for I was quite drunk and do not really know what all he did to me. All I see is me drinking the gin and waking in my own bed the next day. Not caring at all about mom, dad's total focus on her entering the hospital had been on his own enjoyment (the porn) and molesting me.

After that night dad never physically molested me again beyond occasional groping and ogling. That's not to say he didn't try he did. From the next day on (even when he called me to come out to the living room) I moved my bed and dresser in front of my bedroom door at night, so he couldn't get in and continued to do so whenever my mother was away.

Throughout the remaining years of me living at home he did ogle me and say improper things and yes there were still beatings, but he did not ever get the chance to molest me again. The box of porn disappeared when dad went to pick mom up at the hospital.

Mom was in the hospital for over two weeks before the flood damage was cleared enough so she could get home. They had done a surgery of sorts on her without the parts for her knee because the parts never made it to the hospital because of the flood, leaving her partially crippled with no knee cap.

Second memory: Recovery. My mother's recovery at home was long, painful and not without moments of hilarity. Mom's right leg was encased in a cast from hip to ankle and I was her caregiver.

One day shortly after getting home she was laying on the sofa and had to pee. With a little struggle I managed to get a bed pan under her so she could go. The couch being narrow caused her legs to be pressed too close together so that when she started to pee it shot straight up in the air like a fountain! The more she peed the more her and I laughed and the more everything got wet.

We got into many awkward predicaments with mom trying to maneuver in her cumbersome cast. Mom had to do exercises to strengthen the muscles in her leg, one of which was stand between the dining room table and chair and swing her leg while she held on to the table and chair for balance. The cast on her leg was very heavy and unknown to us at the time this exercise caused a muscle in her groin to twist and strangulate.

The pain in mom's groin was passed off as just muscle strain from the exercise. It wasn't long after getting her cast off, in severe pain, with a high fever, mom was taken to the hospital where the twisted muscle was discovered. Already gangrenous with infection having spread to her appendix, mom went into surgery again with me taking on the role of her caretaker once more.

That first surgery proved a catalyst for many more to come. It seemed like whenever mom healed sufficiently from one surgery something else would arise where she again would need surgery. Right knee, groin gangrene, gallbladder, left knee, bowel resection. I was always her main caregiver, dad rarely visiting her in the hospital. Because of the botched first surgery of her right knee mom was unable to work for quite some time and her constant presence in the house the greatest deterrent between my dad and me.

Third memory: Mom on drugs. I believe this incident happened when mom had her gall bladder out as I remember a tube coming out of mom's nose. My brothers and I were visiting mom in the hospital and we had gone down to the machine in the hallway that dispensed little paper cups of soda. We only had thirty-five cents between us which was the price of one cup of soda that we all shared. Coming back into the room we were passing the cup around each taking only one small sip, when spotting us, mom started screaming at us.

"You god damned kids standing there swilling that soda down when they won't let me have a fucking thing!"

Total shock. We had never heard mom swear, ok maybe curse a little like damn or hell but most certainly not the "F" word. We couldn't move, mouths hanging open we just stared. Mom continued to yell and told us to get out of the room and then went on to struggle with the nurse hitting her and swearing.

It was soon discovered that she was having a reaction to the pain medication Demerol. Once the drug cleared her system and new meds administered she was fine. Mom had no memory of anything she had said or done. From that day forward written in bold marker across her medical file was, NO DEMEROL.

Mom was very involved with our church and a member of several organizations within the church so consequently I was too. I went with her everywhere.

I was really the only young person that went to these meetings and I was the adored child of all the little old lady spinsters. I loved them right back they were my peer group as I did not have any social interaction with children my own age. I had a curious mind and I loved hearing or learning anything involving history or about other cultures and the ladies I met at those meetings provided a steady stream of knowledge for me to drink from.

Two of the women that I was particular friends with had met when they were just young girls themselves, meeting in China where one's father had been an advisor to the emperor and the other the daughter of missionaries.

I was never a "child" in the true sense of the word as my innocence had been robbed of me so early and the inner knowledge that welled up in me was so wise, leaving me much more mature than my age. The victim part of me responded as a child but some situations I faced in a very adult manner.

My tastes in music and literature were not in sync with other kids my age. By the age of twelve my passion for reading included books on Edgar Cayce and books written by Ruth Montgomery, anything to do with metaphysical studies. Whenever I read any of this kind of material I felt whole, happy and absolutely fearless, spouting my beliefs to anyone who would listen, even at school.

Normally withdrawn and terrified to talk to anyone at school, if an opportunity came up for me to impart any of my spiritual beliefs I jumped at the chance. I got picked on a lot in school and it hurt me to the core of my being but when I got ridiculed for expressing my spiritual side it did not bother me at all for I was speaking my truth straight from my true self. My spiritual self has always been strong. never weak and scared like my human self, it was many years before I could meld the two aspects and incorporate my spiritual and human selves.

Fourth memory: Grandma's girl. My dad's mother, my grandma, was the only grandmother I ever saw on a regular basis almost daily. Having only had boys she enjoyed doing things with me and for me. Grandma was a very good seamstress and would make me outfits, one particular favorite of mine was a two-piece short and top set made out of yellow calico.

The calico had originally been used for flour bags from days gone by. The memory of this little outfit remained in my mind even though It had been made for me when I was only about seven years old and I remember repeatedly looking for it amongst my things.

Even into my early teens in a daze I would look for this outfit in my dresser going through each drawer and rummaging in my closet. Then suddenly, one day, following another of my futile searches for the outfit the full memory of what had happened to it finally came crashing in.

I had loved the calico outfit so much that I kept on wearing it even when it became too small for me and was a struggle to get on and off. I was wearing it one day when dad molested me and he got mad that it was taking me so long to get the shorts down that he ripped them off me. This day I sobbed not for what was happening to me but because my special present made from flour bags was ruined. Normally I just laid there like a zombie and endured it but this day I cried and I think I even said the dreaded "I Hate You."

For extra punishment (as if being sexually abused wasn't enough) and to cover up the destroyed shorts, after he had finished molesting me, dad made me gather up the remnants of my outfit and had me follow him out to the burning barrel where he made me watch him burn my lovely outfit. Every time I sobbed he would punch me and threaten me that If I didn't shut up he would burn me too.

Mom had to quit working because of her bad knees and dad finished up some college courses he had been taking nights and weekends.

College finished, dad switched to second shift. This was a huge relief for my brothers and I as the only time we had to put up with dad for any length of time was on weekends. Summers were a different story though, even with mom home there was still the verbal and physical abuses suffered while doing outside chores. Thankfully those hours were short lived as he left for work by two.

Dad was somewhat into the metaphysical studies but mom was avid in her quest for more knowledge. With dad at work and we kids old enough to be left without a babysitter mom was able to get together with a group of friends who shared the same interests weekly. They would share books, use the Ouija board, do automatic writing and a couple of them could enter into an altered state and channel. Even though I did not attend the meetings mom shared with me all that happened.

I myself began having prophetic dreams (about close personal connections not global events) and mom would share my dreams or visions with her friends and try and get a group consensus of the meaning. Since I was always with my mother I often had the opportunity to share some of the things I was getting personally with a few of her friends making me feel like an unofficial member of their group.

Fifth memory: The dream. One dream I had took many years even into my adulthood for all the pieces to fall into place. In it I saw a box that looked like a curio shelf sixteen squares four to a row. My mother's friend that lived near us was in the bottom row with members of her family accounted for but one. My mother's friend Olivia, that lived an hour away was in the next row up with one of her family members missing, my mom on the third row with one missing and dad on the top row by himself.

The unfolding of events occurred from the bottom to the top with mom's friend in the lower box going through her crisis first. Parts of the dream explained how the boxes were time frames of when things would happen and the whole comprised an image of the soul connections.

I was in my twenties before all the elements of the dream came together to make an accurate picture. One of the main lessons that came out of the dream was that we are not in truth individual souls but different aspects of a higher soul born to experience similar yet different things.

My mother and her two friends were different character aspects of a common Oversoul, a homemaker, an artist and a scholar. They each lost a son, one to cancer, one to death by an accident and the other to suicide. Although they suffered the same type of loss, losing a son, it was a different process for each of them individually. Collectively, it gave their Oversoul comprehensive data on grief and loss.

I had many prophetic dreams some to be played out in a relatively short period of time and others that have taken many years of my life to unfold. Dreams are not to be confused with Deja-vu they feel different and convey different things.

My prophetic dreams have always been about destiny or something that could not be changed. My Deja-vu dreams are more like reminders to pay attention to what's going on around me, how my actions or words affect the moment I'm in when they occur. In addition to the dreams I practiced ESP (extra sensory perception) even doing an experiment in a science class at school.

For the experiment I chose a classmate to come to the front of the class and whispered in his ear the name of another classmate that I wanted him to concentrate on with me. (I purposely chose a classmate who was not in a popular click.) I waited to see if the person chosen could sense or pick up our thoughts. It worked! I was so excited, the chosen first showed signs by fidgeting, moving his feet and twitching his arms eventually raising his hand and asking if it was him.

I tried many different ESP modalities. I practiced telekinesis by moving small objects like paper clips but was never able to bend a spoon like I saw Uri Geller do on the TV. I also worked with a pendulum and tried my hand at dousing for water.

After my encounter with the UFO when I was eleven I always watched the sky, ever eager to spot another one. My diligence finally paid off, which leads to my next memory event involving a UFO when I was fifteen.

Sixth memory: The big ship. When I was fifteen years old my mom had picked me up after choir practice at our church along with another girl who was a friend and classmate to my younger brother. It was maybe six pm and still fully light out. Mom stopped at the girl's house to let her out and all three of us saw a large spaceship in the sky over in the direction of where our house was located some seven miles away. Excitedly we asked her to call my brother as soon as she got inside and tell him to go outside and look at the space ship and that we (mom and I) would be home in about fifteen minutes.

The ship never moved. I kept my eye on it as we followed the curvy roads in and out of the tree cover. Finally, at the top of a hill less than a mile from home we were right underneath the ship. As we started down the hill the ship finally moved and kept pace with us. At the bottom of the hill we had to make a left turn and OMG the ship followed us! Not afraid, my mom and I were saying how it was like they were waiting for us and had been reading our minds.

We drove the last eighth of a mile and turned into the driveway where my brother and his friend were out in the front lawn watching the ship also. The ship stopped again directly over our house where it stayed a few minutes with us pointing and talking excitedly, when in a blink of an eye it shot out of sight.

I am not sure if anyone else in the area saw that particular ship or not but two weeks later a large ship was spotted in the sky just a little west of our house and remained there for at least forty-five minutes with smaller crafts going and coming from it. Many people saw this one and numerous calls were made to the authorities whose "official" response being it was jets re-fueling in mid-air. I didn't buy it then and I don't buy it now, I know what we all saw, and it wasn't jets.

Seventh memory: The creeper returns. By the time I was 15 it had been quite some time since dad had put his hands on me in a sexual way, though his ogling, physical, mental and emotional abuse continued.

I was mowing lawn one hot summer day with a push mower wearing shorts and a sleeveless Henley style top with a zipper at the neck bordered by a double row of buttons. I had the zipper all the way down due to the heat, showing a fair amount of cleavage as even at that age I was heavy breasted.

I was mowing up alongside the house when I spotted dad at the corner staring at me. I knew that stare only too well and immediately started to pull up the zipper on my shirt. Dad's eyes looked glassy and in the same creepy, child-like, pleading tone that he had used when he had groped me under the table those many years ago he begged me, "please, please don't zip it up."

For a brief moment it looked like he was going to fall to his knees in a classic begging stance, instead with his arms outstretched like a ghoulish zombie, he took a couple of staggering steps towards me still begging me not to pull up my zipper, his eyes brimming with tears. Yes, actual tears.

I was completely repulsed to the point of nausea, the contents of my stomach threatening to come up as at the same time sweat and goosebumps ran down my body. I left the mower where it was and went into the house with my mother. This was the first time he had ever made a sexual advance towards me when mom was home. He clearly was not in his right mind. I never did finish mowing the lawn that day.

- Edgar Cayce 1877-1945 Called "The Sleeping Prophet" an American Christian mystic who performed healings, had prophetic dreams and founded the A.R.E. Association for Research and Enlightenment located in Virginia Beach, VA
- Ruth Montgomery 1912-2001 Journalist and psychic who wrote numerous books on the occult and new age topics
- Uri Geller 1946- Psychic and author of books on psychokinesis and telepathy

CHAPTER 8

Lost

My teenage years were devastatingly sad, not so much because of the abusiveness of dad but because I suffered from deep depression. I've been mystified about people who wish to go back to their teen years and live them again, for me there is not enough money or magic in the world to ever inspire me to go back and live even one day over again.

In my teens I would cry a lot that no one liked me, that I had no friends, aside from my one girlfriend and she was just enough older than me that her life path was leading her away. It didn't help that both my brothers were extremely popular, surrounded by friends and accomplished in sports. Then, there was me, awkward, friendless, the target of ridicule the invisible student.

Sometime when I was in my twenties I recall walking down the main street of my hometown with my mother and we met a former teacher of mine from elementary school. He said hello to my mother and then said, "hello Sophie."

He walked on and I just stood there until my mother turned around and asked me what was wrong. I told her I was amazed he knew who I was. I had felt like such a non-entity, essentially invisible as a child that I really did not think any teacher would ever remember me.

Even though I was sad and desperate feeling about having no friends I could never allow myself to do any of the things that would make me popular or at least acceptable among my peer group. I hated sports and would not attend sporting events. (Probably due to my inability to perform at any and the teasing I had endured when I was younger.) I also would never even consider drinking, smoking pot or doing drugs.

Here is an example of how awkward and ill equipped I was as a teenager. Being close to the river, not far from us, was an area where there were quite a few summer homes and cabins. The neighbor girl was friendly with a boy there for the summer and had been invited to a party, all young people ages 15 to 19. I had been invited by her and after much hesitation I decided to go. Arriving a little late the party was in full swing with everyone drinking alcohol, smoking weed and making out. I showed up carrying a homemade apple pie, need I say more. On a positive note I make awesome apple pie.

Despite the immoral things I endured in my life I had a very moral code of ethics that I applied to everything I did in life. So, I cried a lot, wrote morbid poetry and often thought of suicide but could never surrender to anything that was against my moral ethic, except for sex.

I never dated, never went out with anyone but circumstances did arise where I would be alone with a boy and let's face it most teenage boys will poke anything female that stands still long enough. I did not actively seek sex out, but I never said no.

My programing in that area was do or die, I never struggled never fought back. The sexual victim mindset followed me well into my thirties. I'm very amazed I never contracted a sexually transmitted disease for I had numerous one-night stands and often with men I did not even like. There was no pleasure in sex for me, I just made myself a doormat for men to wipe their boots on.

In a way I suppose my way of dealing with sexual abuse may have been better than the path that other sexual abuse victims had taken. Many women having been sexually abused hate and fear sex and are never fully able to commit to a loving relationship leaving a string of failed relationships or are never even interested in having a relationship.

The opposite side of the coin many sexual abuse victims become promiscuous seeking sex out, often accompanied by drug or alcohol use to drown or deaden any feelings.

I dealt with my abuse somewhere in between., I did not seek just sex and I did not fall into substance abuse to trick my mind into a false sense of bravery. I sought a relationship only I did not know how to approach that ideal other than having sex, with no social skills among boys my own age. I think it was my strong spiritual side that kept me from falling completely into the well of self- loathing.

First memory: First love. There was a boy in school whom I had a mad crush on and in secret I would meet him and we would engage in sexual flirtation not going beyond much more than kissing. I had sex with him once thinking he would fall in love with me, not so. Daily in school I would pass him in the hall walking hand in hand with his perky, popular girlfriend and like any other love-struck teen I was devastated.

Regardless of it only being a clandestine affair I was familiar with his energy and I would know every time I was going to meet him in the hallway weather face on or from behind. I would get a tingling in my fingers first and then a flutter in my stomach. Unlike the vibrational ping I would get when meeting people in passing that gave me a head up as to their character this vibrational signal was decidedly different. This boy was the first boy or even person that I had opened my heart to outside the family.

When you open your heart to someone you allow them to imprint their energy onto you. I'm sure many of you have had a close friend or family member call you on the phone just as you were picking up the phone to call them or visa-versa. Other times you can't get someone out of your mind because something feels off or urgent regarding them. Throughout the years I have imprinted with others but this one was special because he was first.

Second memory: The wind. Occasionally mom would have her best friend over and me included, would use a Ouija board and really get the energy stirred up. On one of these visits we had been using the board seeking the names of our spirit guides. I was fully energized, joyful as always at doing anything metaphysical.

My right hand was on the planchet (the disk that moves around on a Ouija board) and I felt this whirling energy under the palm of my hand as the planchet started spelling out the name, Night Southwind, in fact all three of our hands were being raised off the planchet by the wind emanating from the bottom side of my palm.

All of a sudden, I started spontaneously channeling and said,

"I am Night Southwind your native American guide, I have been with you since birth and I send this wind to help carry you along on your journey."

At this point the wind expanded to encompass the whole dining room swirling around our feet and bringing dust bunnies out from under the china hutch. We three looked at each other in awe until the wind died down, then directed our questions to Night Southwind.

I still have the gift of wind and when I hold my palm over another's palm they can feel the swirling energy. When in a group setting of like-minded people and we are all drawing energy the wind still comes for me and will spin around us raising our energy even higher.

The happy moments like the one just described were not frequent and my normal daily state of mind was deep, oppressive, depression. I would often imagine my funeral and the only one attending would be my mother. I felt like I was a worthless, useless piece of existence, that I was not worthy of being noticed by anyone while alive let alone remembered in death.

I also imagined and wrote out several scenarios for my suicide. Timing and structure had literally been beat into me, so all my suicide plans were carefully planned out for the least amount of mess for someone to have to clean up.

My favorite suicide scenario was me sitting under a spruce tree, up on the hill behind the house, and slitting my wrists, the animals taking care of my body and leaving no trace.

The ultimate happy ending to my suicide fantasies, that while investigating my disappearance they would discover dad's abusiveness and he would be pegged for the crime. Got to love how a depressed teenagers' mind works.

My junior and senior years of high school were the worst. I am often amazed that I maintained a decent grade average considering how often I was just not here in this world mentally.

Third memory: Lost. I am standing in the hallway at school and holding all my books because I can't remember where my locker is. I am sweating and shaking and on the verge of vomiting and crying because I don't remember what class I'm supposed to go to next.

I loiter in the intersection of the two wings where the upper classmen rooms are and wait to see which direction one of my classmates takes so I can follow them to my next class. I'm aware enough to know that I'm in academic and that I have been in the same classrooms with the same classmates since starting high school.

I am the loner, everyone else in small groups shooting the breeze with each other in the few minutes allotted between classes for using the bathroom. I'm afraid to use the bathroom even though I need to pee fearful I might take too long and not have someone to follow.

The blackouts and panic attacks occurred regularly those last two years of school. I took to carting all my books around with me, for often I could not remember where my locker was and if I did remember where it was, I couldn't remember the combination. At other times I would remember the locker number and combination of the locker I had in seventh grade but that was of no use to me. I don't know where I mentally went in between classes, I had to at least be in the present during class as my grades were good.

Maybe I did have a split personality that took over to get me through my classes I don't know. I just always figured I was so depressed that I had blackouts. My regular classes I always made it to because I had someone to follow but I had a few electives that I often missed because I didn't have a familiar person to follow. I would show up at the wrong class on the wrong day and the teacher would say in that tone (you know the tone) "You're not supposed to be here today"

I would back out of the room blushing in embarrassment and find a quiet place to hide until I heard the bell ring. Hearing the bell, I would rush to the main hallway to stalk a classmate to my next destination.

Because of back and knee problems, even at that age, I rarely had to participate in gym class as I usually had a doctor's note to excuse me, instead I helped in the cafeteria and sold milk. There were 3 different lunch periods to accommodate all the students so if I couldn't remember an elective class I would often just go to the cafeteria and help. The teacher of the class I had missed would see me there later and ask why I wasn't in class today, my classic response being "I don't know"

I really didn't know. If there was some trauma that happened to me causing my dissociative state of mind those last two years of school I had no clue then and no clue now, maybe all the awful things I had endured as a child had finally just caught up with me.

I forgot to mention earlier that when I was eleven my older sister, came for her very first visit for her high school graduation present. She came with our grandparents, dad's "real" parents. My sister stayed with me and our grandparents stayed down the road at my other grandparents.

I was so excited, it was love at first sight. We did not go into the circumstances of her being raised on the west coast and me here, she just shared her life with us. It was no surprise to learn that my sister was also very psychically gifted and confirmation for me that psychic abilities ran in families.

With the help of her spirit guides my sister was able to psychically move things around the room and wow her little sister even more. One of the things she shared concerning her abilities was having been challenged by negative beings and people.

My sister told me before leaving that if I ever felt like I was under a psychic attack to mentally call her name and she would be there in spirit to defend me. I had read about dark souls and psychic attacks but did not think that I would ever be a target, I was nobody. In my mind I did not think I mattered in the grand scheme of things, years of "you're stupid, worthless, pitiful" had rendered my self-esteem at near zero. I wasn't worthy of attention from a living person why would a negative entity waste its time on me?

Fourth memory: The attack. I turned eighteen the week after graduating from high school and went to stay with my uncle and aunt (my mother's brother) to look for work as they lived in the suburbs of a city and jobs were more available there then in the country.

I had been there only a few days when shortly after falling asleep one night I was awakened by some force pressing me into the mattress. I was laying on my stomach and a dark coldness was pressing down on me, I couldn't move or speak as my body and face were sinking ever deeper into the mattress and pillow like they were swallowing me whole.

My eyes flew open and I struggled to move, struggled to yell out for my uncle, but all I could manage was a muffled moan of sorts. What my sister had told me years before came to mind and in my head, I yelled her name. Within seconds of calling her name the pressure lifted and my body moved back up several inches. I heard my sister's voice say, "it's all right now."

I must have made some audible sounds in my struggle for my aunt and uncle came to my bedroom, cracked the door and asked if I was alright. I told them I had a nightmare. Needless to say, I was spooked by the incident and even knowing that my sister was only a thought away and dad was still dad, home felt safer, and home I went.

I had since nine years old or so worked. My grandparents owned a store in our local town and I had worked there off and on throughout my childhood and into my teens.

Starting at age eleven I babysat summers for a neighbor and occasionally when they went out. When I was fifteen I started working for another family babysitting at their house in town and also helping at a cousin's pizza shop. My work ethic started young an added incentive being that when I was at work I wasn't at home.

At eighteen I did not want to be under dad's thumb anymore. I stressed to my mother how much I hated dad and I asked to go out to California. I told my mother I could stay with family there, find a job and get to know my sister.

Mom agreed, and within a week I was taxiing down the runway on my first plane trip. Looking out the window as the plane made its way towards the end of the runway I saw my mother clinging to the airport fence, my brothers one on each side and dad standing behind.

I was told later that mom clung to the fence sobbing and calling my name completely hysterical at my leaving. Mom had never recovered from my sister being taken from her and seeing me taking the same route was nearly her undoing, they literally had to pry her loose from the fence.

CHAPTER 9

Independence Can Be scary

I only remember two things of my flight to California, waving goodbye out the window being one. Sometime after takeoff I felt this weird poking in my armpit, moved my arm around a bit and settled into the flight. When the stewardess brought me my dinner she pointed out to me that my underwire from my bra had worked its way out and was sticking out from my sleeve. Complete and total embarrassment for an 18-year-old girl and a trigger for me to disappear.

The remainder of the flight is a mystery as well as who it was that came to pick me up at the airport, I was just there. One minute I'm waving out the plane window to my mom and the next I'm sitting on the bedroom floor in my aunt's house.

First memory: The box. I am sitting on the floor of the bedroom in my aunt's house (dad's oldest sister) and arranging my jewelry box and knick-knacks on the box my clothes were shipped in. I have draped the box with a table cloth to use it like dresser top. I believe at that time I had been there several days but where had I been for those missing days? Even now trying to remember I only see the box.

My aunt was very sweet, and my uncle was a jokester I had met them enough times that I felt comfortable with them. They had one daughter, older than me, and already living on her own, so it was just the three of us.

Second memory: Scene straight out of a movie. My aunt and uncle at work I put on nice clothes and did my makeup and hair and set out on foot to go job hunting. My aunt's house was only a few blocks from the main avenue leading to Disneyland and there were multiple businesses located there.

I had just put my application in at one restaurant and was heading up the street to another restaurant when a car pulls up alongside me. The car was a big, long Cadillac, the dashboard fur trimmed and there was dingle ball fringe framing the windshield and rear window. I heard a voice calling me, "hey lady, hey pretty lady, where you goin'?"

Unfolding from the car was a tall, lanky black man. The man was a pimp. Dressed in the street garb of the 70's: velvet sport coat with the oversize satin lapels, shiny silk trousers and a wide brimmed hat trimmed with a satin band and feather. With a smile as wide as Texas, he tried to recruit me as a prostitute.

Apparently, I was heading into his territory and my new girl in town, country bumpkin, fresh meat status, stuck out like a sore thumb. To me he looked like he had just stepped off the set of "The Mod Squad" or some other TV crime series of the day. Backing away and mumbling no thanks I turned and ran back to the house, probably the fastest I've ever moved in my life.

I did not stay long with this aunt for her and her husband were having problems plus she thought I would be happier staying with my other aunt her younger sister whose three kids, my cousins, were the same ages as my brothers and me.

My cousins and I had known each other as children, they had lived about an hour away from us and we visited regularly. I remembered fun times at their house playing hide and seek among the farm buildings. One time when they visited us one of my cousins and I were arguing over which one of us was more country. We challenged each other by walking through a stubble field bare foot, I was ready to quit after about two feet, it really hurt, but I toughed it out. Our challenge ended in a draw with us each suffering bruised and bleeding feet.

Not long after that visit my aunt divorced her husband (he was a violent drunk) and taking my cousins moved to California to be nearer to her siblings and parents. By the time I arrived and became reacquainted with my cousins they had been living out there long enough that the "country" had worn off and they lived happy, busy lives in suburbia.

After moving in with my aunt and cousins I quickly found a job in a pizza parlor a few blocks away. I remember how excited I was at my first paycheck taping it in a scrapbook I was keeping of my adventure in the land of sunshine. I spent as many weekends as I could (work allowing) with my sister, plus she came and visited me.

My aunt had a good-sized house with a sunken living room that was three steps down and extending the full length of the back of the house. My sister had warned me about the living room telling me that there was an evil/negative force out there and not to sit out there by myself, but she did not go into details and I did not heed her warning.

Third memory: Invisible threat. Home alone one day I left my bedroom and wandered out to the living room drawn by the sunlight streaming in the windows and the beauty of the trees in the back yard. I sat there watching TV when an eerie coldness came over me and I felt a hot breath on the back of my neck accompanied by a strange whispering in my ear which grew into a shout of "you're mine now!"

Jumping up in panic I headed to the doorway when suddenly my arm was grabbed by invisible fingers nearly jerking me off my feet. I managed to pull away and sprinted to the doorway where upon entering the kitchen everything stopped. Whatever it was it could not or would not leave the living room.

The entity did not bother anyone if there was more than one person in the room only those in there alone. I had bruise marks of a hand print on my arm that lasted a week. My sister told me of a similar attack that had happened to her in which after hearing the threatening voice she ran for the doorway only to have the entity grab her on the steps by the ankle and try to drag her back into the room. My sister said she really had to struggle to break free and was left with hand marks around her ankle.

Fourth memory: The bullet. My aunt's house was only a few blocks away from the plaza where the pizza shop was that I worked at. Once I left the quiet street my aunt lived on I had to walk along a very busy main avenue until I reached the plaza.

Walking home one day after work I heard the sound of a gunshot and felt the WIZ of a bullet pass right in front of my face only to smack into the wall of a bowling alley that I was walking past. Intended for me or for a passing vehicle I do not know? What I do know is that I have amazing guardians watching over me and a very tight sphincter muscle!

My sister took me to meet our father, I had such high hopes that he would love me and want to be a part of my life. Boy was I wrong, he did not want anything to do with me. When my father had moved to California he remarried and forged a new life and did not want any reminders of his other life and I came with lots of baggage.

I seem to recall that I had written him a letter once begging him to rescue me, but not sure if I really did write it or just thought about writing one. Either way I was not wanted by him and it was a hurt that I handled very well because I did not remember him, there were no memories or feelings attached to him. I met him two other times before I left California and they were by accident, just chance meetings.

My grandmother was still working and I had put an application in at her place of employment. I was hired there so I quit the pizza shop to work in the factory. I rode back and forth to work with my grandmother giving us a chance to know each other better because I only knew her from a few visits she had made back east.

I could not weave the two images of my grandmother together in my head. The party hearty, bar hopping, bar owning, wife swapping, young mother who tried to abort her last child six times and the mild mannered, working 60 plus hours a week, woman setting next to me.

The crowning achievement of my grandmother's younger self (as she related it my older brother some years later, while visiting,) was her and our grandfather stopping and having sex 13 times along a 60 mile stretch of highway.

My grandmother had also shared a story with me a few times after she moved back to PA and was quite elderly at the time. (I know I was in my 40's at the time) She told me that as a young high school girl she had walked to her girlfriends' house after school and it was really hot out. Grandma related that she was miserable hot and sore because she had just shaved her "pussy" the night before and had prickly heat rash. When I was in high school I didn't even know women did such a thing.

I had only worked at the factory a few months when I decided to go back home. I was a little homesick for my mother and even though I dreaded being under the same roof as dad again I kept having a feeling or "knowing" that my path was there in so I returned home.

CHAPTER 10

Shame on Me

It was the tail end of winter when I arrived back home in and I quickly found a job at a local sub and pizza shop that was close to the factory where dad worked. I worked the evening shift and became friendly with a group of people near my age that came in frequently on their supper hour break from the factory.

Thursdays were payday and I would meet my friends after work at a local bar that was not very diligent checking ID's. I find it amusing that the few months of my life that I actually drank (moderate at that) I wasn't even legal. By the time I was legally able to drink I had no interest in drinking. I really had a good time with my new-found friends and began shedding layers of shyness and awkwardness.

I was still living at home but saving every penny I could in anticipation of having my own place. The lure of getting out from under the same roof as my dad curtailing any thoughts of using my pay for anything other than my car payment and gas. Any false sense I may have harbored of me being able to stay longer than necessary in his house came crashing in one afternoon.

First memory: The soap opera. My new job at the pizza shop was afternoon hours as were the jobs my dad and brother had. After lunch we would all sit and watch tv until it was time for us all to leave for our respective jobs. In those days there was not the television programming of today, it was either a game show or a soap opera.

We had all become interested in a particular soap that was on the hour before we all had to leave. The three of us were sitting there watching the current episode unfold…. One of the main female characters was having a mental breakdown upon remembering being molested and raped by her father.

I froze. I couldn't move. I was sitting closest to the tv, dad and my older brother behind me. I gripped the arm of the chair so they wouldn't see me shaking, sweat began pouring down my body and my stomach was threatening to become a volcanic eruption. I wanted to melt into the chair, shame, horror, embarrassment and overwhelming panic made it impossible to move to barely breath.

Were they looking at me, did my brother even remember me telling him of the abuse. Would the scene unfolding on television inspire dad to try and assault me again? My thoughts were spinning out of control when I heard dad speak.

"They should cut his balls off. Any man who would do that to his daughter should be killed."

I sat there in stunned silence. How could he say something like that, what about him, what about what he had done to me? It was like there was no memory in him of his abuse of me. Was he truly believing what he had just said or was it for the benefit of my brother?

I was aghast. (the perfect word of how I felt). The show ended and we all got up to leave for our jobs, my legs shaky and weak I stumbled out to my car and sat there dazed and unmoving for some time.

I had become good friends with a girl from the factory, talking on her lunch hour and hanging out at the bar after work. Shortly after the tv incident I moved in with her, I could not wait to escape from my parent's house and from all the shameful memories there. My friend had a cabin in the woods and it seemed a grand adventure to live without conveniences. I remember cooking a 3-course meal on a Coleman stove, and inviting guests to dinner.

Second memory: The accident. I was already in bed one night when my friend came in late from work and asked me to get dressed and come for a ride in her jeep. I threw something on and we took off cruising back roads with her friend driving. I did not know he was drunk and the next thing I knew we were careening off the road and the jeep was rolling. With no top on the jeep I was thrown out and came to consciousness laying in the middle of the road.

We had wrecked not far from a house and hearing the accident the people living there called an ambulance and we were all transported to the hospital. In pain and scared I called my parents from the hospital to find they were already up.

My dad at the precise moment of the accident had heard what to him sounded like a stick of dynamite going off in his head and waking, he knew something had happened to me.

Why of all the people I knew did the person I hated the most in the world have that strong of an awareness of me? What was our spiritual connection? Had I orchestrated the unnatural alliance between us before coming into this life?

The thought that I might have agreed to and helped set up my own abuse made me hate myself even more. At this point in my life I was still learning how reincarnation and life lessons worked. I was not able to see the whole picture, all I could think of at that time was that, "I" had agreed to it, and "I" hated, "me"

I was pretty banged up from the accident and as if my ass hadn't had enough trauma from my childhood, when I got flung out of the jeep I landed on it. Along with a butt bruised to the bone I had a concussion and road rash. At the ER they had been so focused on a possible back injury (because that's where I complained of the most pain) that the concussion was missed and they never cleaned my wounds.

Mom and dad took me home to convalesce where mom had to soak my road rash with hot, wet, towels, to loosen everything up and remove all the grit with tweezers. For the better part of a week every time I stood up unassisted I passed out. It took me several weeks to heal from the accident so I had been replaced at work.

It didn't take me long to find another job. The job I found was working in a half-way house for alcoholics. I was basically a part-time baby sitter and part-time cook. One of my duties was to dole out vitamins for the clients who all were in various stages of detoxing their bodies from alcohol and do intake paperwork for sad souls coming in from the street.

The mentally ill and cross addicted clients that made their way through our doors we only held for a short period of time until we could transport them to a more qualified facility.

Working the night shift, I got into a situation where a client made advances on me and my "victim" status kicked in and we had sex. The client mentioned it to the house counselor in a therapy session and next thing I knew I was fired. The only job I ever got fired from, I was nineteen. This is the first time I have ever revealed why I left that job, not even my closest friends knew, I was too embarrassed.

While I was still employed at the half-way house my friend and I moved out of her cabin and rented an actual apartment with all the modern conveniences, the glow having worn off roughing it at the cabin. We only shared the apartment a short time it just didn't work for us there, each wanting to be top dog we argued but remained friends and she moved back home.

There was a guy I really liked, another member of the group I hung out with. I can't say that we dated beyond meeting up at the bar but we spent time together and as per usual we became lovers. Even though I felt like I was falling in love with him I still had sex with some else at the same time. Another friend, drunk, on his way home would stop at my apartment and pressure me into having sex. I did not put up too much resistance at the first hint of coercion I would crumple like a paper doll and just allow it to happen.

I could not fight for myself, courageous in other areas of my life, I continued to let myself be victimized. Instead of fighting back and saying no, I just wallowed in shame and guilt.

CHAPTER 11

Humor, Horror and Happiness

I loved having my own place and when I got fired I found another job as quickly as possible so I would not have to surrender my new-found freedom. I started working at a diner that stayed open 24 hrs. Thursday through Saturday to cater to all the drunks with the munchies at 2 am when the bars closed.

First memory: Bottoms up. One evening getting off work at 11 pm I went out to my car and was greeted by the sight of a couple having sex in the parking lot. Their car was parked very close to mine and the passenger side front door of their car was open.

The girl was sprawled on the front seat and her boyfriend was banging away at her, butt cheeks highlighted by the parking lot lights. The guy must have been quite tall as his feet were against my car door and I couldn't get my door open. I tried, "Ahem, and excuse me" but to no avail, he just kept pumping away.

I went back inside and told the town cop (who was in for a coffee break) and a few friends what was going on in the parking lot and we all went out outside where the officer shone a flashlight on them, but they just kept at it seemingly oblivious to their audience. Laughing, we all went back inside shaking our heads in disbelief that such a thing could happen and drank more coffee.

A bit later the couple walked in the door and ordered breakfast, eyes bright with the afterglow of sex, alcohol and whatever drug they had been using. Between their obviously high state and nonchalant attitude we figured they were indeed completely unaware that we had all been witness to their prolonged encounter.

Leaving early from work one night I went up to the bar to meet up with my friends. It was Thursday night, payday for the factory workers and my dad's binge night.

Second memory: Public embarrassment. My dad was holding court with his cronies at one end of the bar when I went to the opposite end to order a soda because I was going to go back to work to cook for the bar crowd later. My dad spying me points his finger my way and at the top of his voice so everyone at the bar could hear he shouted, "look at the tits on that one."

I thought I would die right there. Tears running down my face I left the bar and went back to the diner, shut myself in the walk-in cooler and cried my eyes out. Everyone at the bar knew I was his daughter, what would they all think and what if in his drunkenness he told his drinking buddies about molesting me?

The owner of the diner came in the cooler as he had seen me run in and I told him what my dad had said stating, "how could he do that to me I'm his daughter?"

He told me not to worry about it, it was just the alcohol talking and everyone would dismiss it as that. But he did not know my whole story, my horror, that my shame might be made public.

I just remembered another incident at the same bar only this one occurred before I had moved out of my parent's house. My car was broken down and I had to ride to work with dad. It happened to be a Thursday, so we went to the bar after work.

I was hanging with my friends when I noticed that dad was gone and it still was rather early. I sought out dad's oldest friend and he told me that dad had asked him to give me a ride home. When my dad's friend was driving me home he told me that my dad not only asked him to give me a ride but also to have sex with me.

Daddy Dearest, essentially, tried to pimp me out. Even more tragic it was not for money, he only wanted details. Dad thought if he offered me up on a silver platter his friend would jump at the chance. Dad's friend was more of a gentleman than he knew, I was escorted safely home.

I have always been thankful when a happy, funny or joyful memory followed closely on the heels of a traumatic one. I was trying very hard to pull myself out of the quagmire of depression that I had been stuck in most of my life, it did not take much for me to be sucked back into it because my self-esteem remained very low.

Third memory: Flying pizza. The owner of the diner came up with the brilliant idea of putting in a pizza oven as if 24 hr. food wasn't enough. It might not have been such a challenge except that he wanted to use fresh dough that you had to stretch and hand toss to form the crust. To my misfortune I was the only employee who could get the pizza crust into any kind of circular shape, so the owner's solution was to only offer pizza on the nights I was working.

One night not another soul showed up for work except me, leaving me to be chief cook, dishwasher and waitress. The grill area was open to the counter but the pizza table was in the back and I had an order for a pizza. Twirling the pizza on the back of my hands I kept stepping to the doorway to keep an eye on the customers and shouting my, "I'll be right there I'm almost done"

When all of a sudden, the pizza dough went sailing off my hands out the door like a miniature UFO where it skidded along the counter and wiped out six customers plates and cups. Tears running down my cheeks from laughter I went about cleaning up the mess to cheers and applause from the patrons. My heart became a little lighter that day when I realized that if I did something wrong I would not be beat or verbally chastised for it.

Among my fellow employees at the diner was a man 11 year older than me. Tim was quiet, kind, hardworking, and I felt comfortable and safe around him. Though I did not recognize or remember him he had been a resident at the half-way house when I worked there and was a recovering alcoholic.

We talked a lot at work and went to the laundromat together, but we never dated. I had a bit of a crush on him and felt that he really liked me too. Tim lived in an apartment at the other end of town that was also owned by our employer.

Our boss, a twenty plus years veteran of sobriety helped other alcoholics by giving them an inexpensive place to live while they got their lives back in order. Tim shared an apartment there with another guy who quickly went off the wagon, so he asked me if he could move in with me to get away from the situation, I said yes.

Fourth memory: Breaking the ice. Nervous and unsure of how I was to proceed in my new living arrangement I offered Tim the bed and I slept on the couch. Given my habit of just falling into bed with anyone this was a HUGE step for me. I was then and still being very practical in my approach to things, the next morning I sat on the couch making a list of things we would need to support two people.

Engrossed in my list I did not notice Tim walk into the room from the bedroom until, as passing me on his way to the kitchen he said, "don't mind me."

I Looked up to the sight of his bare ass going through the doorway. I was too shocked to speak, he laughed and said, "one of us had to break the ice."

Several months later he asked me to marry him and I said yes. His manner of asking me to marry him was cute and funny and I still smile when I recall it. We were lying in bed one morning and he asked me, "have you ever thought about getting married?"

I replied yes, then he said, "to me you know."

I still laugh as if I would think of marrying someone else when laying in his arms. Too funny. When I told my sister over the phone about my engagement she asked me if I loved him I told her I wasn't sure but that I knew I was supposed to marry him.

We both got new jobs and moved into a house his parents owned in the country and married in February less than a year after meeting. Our income was not the greatest so two months after we were married my husband left for Texas for a job his brother had arranged for him there. Tim saved money for an apartment for us by living with his brother.

A couple of months later, car loaded down like a gypsy caravan, I made my first solo, long drive cross country. I was happily surprised at how friendly the people were that I met along the way, especially when tragedy struck.

Fifth memory: Heartbroken. I had stopped at the Texas welcome rest area on I 10 to go to the bathroom. I was traveling with not just all our stuff but also my 2 cats. Temperatures in the car were not too bad without air conditioning while moving but at a standstill it was oppressive. Leaving the windows cracked for my 2-minute dash to the restroom I returned to get in the car and one cat got out. I caught him and put him back in the car. Not happy about it he clawed my chest.

I went to start the car and nothing, no juice. I had to get back out to get help and after finding someone I open the car door and they both get out. It was 110 degrees that day and they did not want any part of that broken-down car.

I spent the better part if an hour trying to catch them but no luck. There was a nice couple that got my car started for me and led me to a service station off the highway. Before leaving, the staff at the rest area gave me a number for an animal rescue that worked the rest areas as many people lost pets at them.

Car fixed for the moment I drove the last miles to my destination, sobbing all the way. Upon arriving at my brothers-in-law's house, I again called the rescue but nothing. For a month I called daily but they were never seen. For years I imagined them traveling back home, a fantasy that was much more to my liking then the other alternatives, a 10- lane highway on one side and an alligator ridden bayou/swamp on the other. I preferred the fantasy.

I was able to find work quickly in Texas, but I was never happy there. I ran into a lot of prejudice there against northerners and was bullied by my coworkers. Even though I was raised in a small town where minorities were a rare thing I had no prejudice. I accepted people for who they were not the color of their skin, their religious belief or location they came from.

I did not have problems with the ethnic people I worked with but with the white coworkers. I warn you this next memory is offensive on many levels and has stuck with me ever since, but it needs to be told as I experienced it.

Sixth memory: The Civil war isn't over. I was hired as a prep cook and the chef was a wonderful and talented black woman, Miss Izzy. Miss Izzy ran her kitchen with a firm hand but fairly, without preferential treatment to her own race, we were all equals.

It was a cafeteria style eatery and prep work done me and my coworkers went out and helped serve on the food line as people filed past with their trays. I was stationed in between 3 white men and when customers weren't within hearing range they made racist and disparaging comments about our chef.

One day noticing I was not agreeing or commenting and frankly looking very uncomfortable, the man on my left leaned into me a bit and said, "one thing us Texans hate worse than a bus load of niggers is a car with a Pennsylvania license plate"

I was appalled. Getting no response from me they started sabotaging my work area making messes so I would get blamed for it. I felt that if I said anything to management it would only make it worse. In southern Texas you don't go up against "the good ole boys" and get away with it. Quitting my job seemed like a much better option.

At our apartment complex when I tried doing laundry at the laundromat I had stones thrown at me and could not go there by myself but had to wait for my husband to go with me. The straw that broke the camel's back still stands out in my mind.

Seventh memory. Hold-up. It was a Saturday evening around 8 pm when Vincent and I decided we wanted some ice cream. I walked over to a convenience market that was across the street from our apartment complex to buy some. I was in the back of the store at the freezer section when a man came in the door of the store brandishing a hand gun. Firing off one round he points the gun at the cashier demanding money. Me and several other customers crouched down behind shelving units too scared to even cry watching while it all play out.

The cashier a Vietnamese man, totally calm, gives the man the money from the drawer while calling the police with the other hand. He was so used to this happening he never broke a sweat. My fear must have triggered one of my disappearing acts because the next thing I remember is standing in my apartment, minus the ice cream, telling my husband what had happened and stating, "I want to go home."

The next day I called the restaurant where I had been working before we moved to Texas and talked to the manager there that I had remained friends and asked her if there would be a job for me if I came home. There was. That was the end of my stay in Texas, I lasted 9 months.

Funny, I don't remember if I flew home or drove home, my next coherent thought is of me standing in the living room of the trailer I rented after coming back home. I must have stayed with someone until I had enough money to rent the trailer, but it is just a blank, I am just there with the knowing that my husband would be there in about two weeks now that we had a place live.

We did not stay long in the trailer but moved back into the house his parents owned even though it was a 50-minute drive one-way, figuring it was cheaper to buy gas to drive the extra distance then it was to pay rent.

Like most young married couples, we wanted children and not long after getting resettled in the farm house I missed my first cycle. When two more months rolled around, and I again did not have my period I went to the doctor and after a physical exam the doctor said my uterus was rounded and I looked pregnant. I was in pig heaven. Heading into my fourth month my period started as usual with no visible signs of a miscarriage. This same scenario would repeat itself several more times and each false pregnancy another piece of my heart would be shattered.

Seventh memory. The examination. I am in a sparkling white room, walls, floors and ceiling the whitest white I had ever seen. There are several shelves protruding from the walls, they are rectangular measuring approximately three feet wide by two and a half feet deep and are about four feet up from the floor.

I am standing on one facing the wall and I am naked. I am instructed to squat down by a short alien being. The position I am in exposes and opens up my genital area for examination by the alien being. I feel no sense of fear and have total recall of the event the next day.

I called my mother and told her about the exam, excitedly telling her that I think the extraterrestrials did it to fix something so I could have children. There was not then or now any doubt in my mind that this was an alien abduction scenario, considering all the extraterrestrial visits I had witnessed and the episodes of missing time I had experienced.

I never did get pregnant or more accurately carry a pregnancy to full term. It was not until about a year ago while watching a tv documentary about alien interactions with humans that I came to a different understanding of what my extraterrestrial examination may have been.

The program featured several women who had experienced abductions while pregnant and through hypnosis recalled their embryos being taken by the aliens. I now also believe this is what happened to my missing pregnancies. Can I prove it? No, but it feels right. Maybe someday I will get clarification, but for now this is my theory.

CHAPTER 12

Life and Loss

One day while my husband and I were visiting with our friend Matt, he told us of an employment boom going on in Massachusetts and asked us if we would be interested in going there to look for work. Discussing it with family and since none of us were getting full time hours and only making minimum wage with no benefits, we decided to take the risk of traveling out of state again for better wages and good benefits. With high hopes and only a suitcase of clothes each, five of us set out for the unknown, me, my husband, my older brother our friend Matt and one of his friends.

Arriving in Massachusetts we found a motel room with 4 beds and a kitchenette, sharing the expenses while we looked for work. We all found work in less than 2 weeks the various companies eager to hire us on telling us that they liked hiring people from rural communities because we were hard workers.

Our next move was to an apartment we again shared until we all had enough money to get our own places. That first apartment we all shared was a doozie, it was a fourth-floor walk-up and there were no appliances! I remember we had a Styrofoam cooler we put ice in everyday to keep our food cold and I cooked for us all with a Betty G fry cooker, an old electric frying pan with a broken leg you had prop up with something and a coffee pot. I felt like I had started a new fad, "high rise camping!"

The first weekend off after everyone's first pay, the guys made a quick round trip home to bring back mattresses for everyone so that even though we were sleeping on the floor we were somewhat comfortable. Luckily our rent was by the week, so we didn't have to live there long before we all had saved enough money to acquire permanent living quarters.

Me, my husband and my brother found a nice apartment with quirky oddball nooks and crannies in it which appealed to my own quirky nature, the only downfall it was a third-floor walk-up but better than the fourth floor we had vacated. Our other friends also found an affordable home and brought up the rest of their family. Life went on, work, new friends and before we knew it a full year had passed and things were really good…Until.

In March of 1984, my brother decided to make a spur of the moment trip to Pennsylvania to visit his children and my husband went along for the ride to visit his brother. I could not go as it was my weekend to work at my job.

First memory. Sunday morning, I am getting ready for work and I hear the door open and my husband walks in with some woman with him. He points at me and flicking his finger in the direction of our bedroom, tells me to go there.

Panicked and confused at this point I turn to go, a hundred thoughts running through my mind. Who is with him, how did he get here, is he leaving me for this other woman?

When we get into the bedroom my husband asks me to sit on the bed and then proceeds to tell me that my younger brother had been killed in an accident the day before and that he had asked his sister-in-law to ride along with him so she could drive me back home thinking I would be too upset to drive and knowing he would not be able to get the week off to take me.

I could not wrap my mind around the news and remember only a feeling of relief that it was my sister-in-law standing in the kitchen and not a mistress. I really had not recognized her standing behind him everything seem surreal.

I had to call my boss to say I would not be in for the rest of the week and when telling him the reason why, reality hit and I started sobbing, too incoherent to say anything further I handed the phone to my husband. Hastily gathering some clothes together, I left. I don't think my sister-in-law even got a chance to do more than pee.

The trip home for my brother's funeral seemed to take forever. I asked to share the driving, but my sister-in-law had promised Tim not to let me drive, they both feared I would have a breakdown. Surprisingly I was calm, more concerned for my sister-in-law making the trip back with only a few moments break from being in the car.

It was quite late when I arrived at my parent's house, but everyone was awake. Upon seeing me my mother had a complete melt down. I learned the details of the accident, realizing as I did so, that I had driven over the exact spot where my sweet brother had lost his life on the way to my parents not 10 minutes ago.

My brother had been on his way home from work on his and was coming through a small village only a few miles from home when a car coming the opposite direction took a left turn up a side street cutting him off. My brother crashed head on into the passenger side of the car.

The driver of the car had been drunk, a local, known alcoholic, who had been involved in other drunken vehicular mishaps over the years. You can't get away with a crooked fart in small rural communities, everyone knows everyone's business. We country folk didn't need Facebook then, Ma Bell, was gossip central and any mishap anyone was involved in made the rounds before the object of that gossip ever made it back to their home.

Second memory: Mom's dream. This memory is of a dream my mother had and had shared it with me and of a dream I had that went along with it. My mom's father was in ill health and for the past year or so she had been going to my grandfather's house and staying several days during the week and her siblings on alternating weekends.

One night in the late fall or early winter at her father's house my younger brother had appeared to my mom in a dream. Mom said he had been covered in blood and his face and chest had been mutilated. When I heard the details of my brother's accident and death, the memory of the dream my mom had told me about instantly popped into my mind. The way my brother had appeared in the dream was how my brother looked according to witnesses after the accident.

Somehow, someway my brother's death had been preordained. Did my mom have a prophetic dream telling her of events to come, or did my brother's higher self, come to my mother to help prepare her for what was to come? Both are gone now so there is no way to discover the origin of the dream. My mother and brother were both highly spiritual beings it could have been either. Our pre-life choices the greatest mystery we will ever encounter in our lives.

Just two months before he had been killed my brother had also been in another very bad car accident, rolling his van which had landed on its roof collapsing it like an accordion. We believe what had saved him from dying that time is that his best friend was in the vehicle with him and it was not his friends time to go.

Third memory: My dream. I had also had a dream at the exact same time as my mother had, had hers. In the dream I was at my grandfather's house (my mom's father) and someone with a machete had cut off my grandfather's hand.

I am trying to staunch the bleeding and I'm calling 911 but I keep getting a busy signal. When I finally I get through and they tell me they are sending out an ambulance. In my mind's eye I see the ambulance being prevented from arriving by multiple things, a train, an accident and so on.

What I got from the dream is that no matter what I did death was going to happen. Death was inevitable, a planned timely occurrence. I knew that my mom's dream and mine were connected, each dreaming of death at the exact moment.

This was to be the first of my "death dreams" all very bloody and graphic in their violence. I find this strange even though I have a very vivid imagination, I do not like that kind of content in books or movies.

Over the years I have figured out that if the death blow or injury is by knife or machete a family member is going to die, become dangerously ill or hurt, but I never know who. In other death dreams, death or injury has been by a rifle and in these cases, it is someone non-related to me but very close.

I still have these bloody dreams and I am just as unable to tell who the dream is specifically about now, as I was then, only knowing if it is family or a friend by weapon. OMG! I just think I figured something out. The representation of a knife being what kills family in my death dreams, is related to my attempts to kill dad with a knife. Duh, only took me 30 years to figure it out.

In the days leading up to the funeral my mother shared with me all the supernatural and miraculous things that had occurred from the moment my brother had died. My brother had recently gotten engaged and he appeared to his fiancé and her sister wearing an off-white sport jacket that he always wore. Upon seeing him the sister said, "what are you doing here?" only to have him disappear.

While family and friends gathered at my parent's house only hours after the accident and shared their sorrow all the interior lights and headlights came on in the cars parked in the driveway for several moments. My brother saying his goodbyes and letting everyone know that he was ok.

Throughout the years since my younger brother's passing me and mom and sometimes me alone had tried to contact my brother but never succeeded. It is like he came into this life for a purpose, accomplished it and went on. My little brother's soul was so pure he left no karmic footprint, that is not to say he wasn't missed he was, but his higher-self felt no need to linger on the earthly plane.

I did not know the "man" who had died. The last time I saw my brother he was 18 and had just joined the navy and attended my wedding in his uniform. My brother still looked a boy then, smooth skinned and innocent. He was away at sea while I was busy traipsing around the United States with my husband.

My brother did not get his full growth until he was 21 yrs. old, after which he shot up and out making it impossible for him to even do the job he was trained for on a submarine. In fact, my brother got out of the navy on a medical discharge because he got so big.

I am glad I was not around him in his adult physique because it was not just his size that changed his looks did too, he became the spitting image of dad. It was a closed casket due to all the damage to his face and I only saw what he had looked like at the time of his death by recent photos. I was able to mourn the boy I had loved and not be troubled by the face of the monster I hated.

The funeral over and things settled as well as they could be, me and my older brother traveled back to Massachusetts. We talked a lot during the trip, (probably more than we ever had) about our brother and our childhood.

I went into a little more detail about my sexual abuse telling my brother that "dad would send you boys outside to play so he could be alone with me."

Dead silence in the car, until with tears in his eyes, my brother said he finally believed me about the abuse because dad never let him go play.

My brother has a memory that stretches to the womb and he was able to recall times that dad had sent him and our younger brother out to play without me. I'd like to say that clearing the air, so to speak, made us closer but it didn't, something has always made it uneasy between us.

A few months after the funeral the company where my brother worked moved and he moved with the company. Although he moved less than 40 miles away, there were many more miles than that between us.

After my brother moved out I also felt the need for change and took a new job as a kitchen manager at a big Texas style BBQ restaurant and bar. It didn't take me long to realize that being paid, "salary" was just a nice way of saying, "you're screwed now, and we own you 70 hrs. a week."

While I was sweating my butt off and killing myself in the kitchen, the owner, bar manager and their friends were in the office doing lines of cocaine, which I interrupted one day when I went in to ask for help in the kitchen. I gave my 2 weeks' notice at the end of my shift.

I decided I had, had enough of busting my tush in restaurants. I believe it was fear more than anything that kept me working in restaurants, it was familiar, something I knew how to do. Although I was fearless about moving and discovering new places, I was terrified of trying new jobs out of fear of being ridiculed. The years of being beat and shamed for doing a chore incorrectly made me consistently gravitate towards something I knew how to do so I wouldn't look stupid or incompetent.

With much apprehension and a stomach full of butterflies I applied for my first non-kitchen job at the factory where my husband worked.

CHAPTER 13

Copper Fleas and Ghosts

The industry boom that had brought us to Massachusetts, was circuit boards. The computer age had arrived, and everyone was cashing in on the abundance of jobs. I got hired quickly, experience not needed, as everyone was learning something new for the technology was changing daily.

First memory: First impression. My first day of work I was so nervous I could barely walk my legs were shaking and my stomach was churning. The supervisor escorted me to the door of the room I was to work in, pointed through the window to a girl sitting at a desk and told me her name was Kay and that she would be my group leader and would show me what to do.

It was a clean room environment and I had to get dressed in white coat and put on a hairnet. I entered the room in full panic my pallor, whiter than the smock I was wearing and said hi. Kay turned to me and said, "I don't remember what your name is"

Trying to overcome my fear I thought I would be witty and replied, "my name is Sophie, but I'll answer to anything, you can call me an ignorant slut if you want too."

Her eyes popped and she started laughing hysterically to the point she fell out of her chair and unto the floor. From that point on we became the best of friends.

Kay told me a few days later that she had told her dad about me telling him her first impression of me was not too favorable. Stiff and scared looking upon entering the room she did not think I would last the day until I dropped my zinger.

Referring to myself in such a negative way was, sadly, another comfort zone for me. Making fun of myself was less hurtful than having someone else do it. By presenting myself as worthless I lowered her expectations of me so anything I screwed up on would seem in keeping with my self-portrayed ignorance.

I loved my job. My childhood lessons in proper procedure and timing, brutal though they were, had made me a great employee no matter what the job. The ability to prepare a meal with everything coming together at the right time, one of the things that made me a good cook. These same attentions to detail and the need to "do it right" the first time, made me a valuable asset in my work environment.

Initially I balked at cross training in different departments copping a pissy attitude when asked to do something different than what I was used to. I was so fearful of looking stupid that I would get grumpy and mean to mask how terrified I was at the thought of making an error in front of someone. The memory of dad's fist punctuating my errors one thump at a time a contributing factor in my approach to any task.

The circuit board shop where I worked that first time was located in a massive old mill building situated alongside a river, where prior to the Civil war it had processed raw cotton from the south. There were at least 5 stories above ground and 2 basement levels, sturdy brick walls and massively thick timbers held it all together.

The building also had its share of ghosts; safety precautions were pretty much non-existent in these old mills and deaths and injuries were very common place back in the early days of milling.

Second memory: Peekaboo I see you. My first encounter with, "the working man ghost" happened shortly after I started. Besides the huge beams that supported the building there were several circular steel posts adding their support in the large open areas.

One day upon leaving my work room I started out across a large open space and saw a figure peeking around one of the steel posts, he was wearing dark blue pants and a lighter blue men's work shirt. I think he was shocked that I saw him, his eyes widened, and he disappeared.

I saw the working man ghost frequently and his favorite spots were leaning with his back against one of the many steel posts with one leg bent so his foot rested against the post too, a perfectly nonchalant pose. (I'm not sure why, but the working man ghost followed me to whichever company I worked at over the next 10 years or so. Only factory jobs.) It was a very large building and work areas were spaced quite some ways apart, and my ghostly friend seemed to follow me to whichever area I traveled to. The encounters were brief, just long enough that I knew he was there and he never tried to communicate with me other than by appearing.

A lot of the technology has changed now but at that time circuit boards were made by taking sheets of a fiberglass resin and covering it with a thin sheet of copper which was then cut into squares or rectangles.

Once cut, the boards were coated with a photographic material and my job was to take an artwork image of circuits apply it to the panel and place the individual panels into a machine that exposed it to light like a camera. These were the first few steps in building a board and each step had its hazards and problems.

In the very first stage of cutting the boards to size a pile of rough edges, copper and fiberglass shavings would pile up and some kind of flea would take up residence in the shavings. You wouldn't think a flea would be attracted to a pile of shavings, but they were, and we all got bit, our legs would be covered in flea bites whenever in that area. This was not a phenomenon to this one shop, I worked in several other circuit board shops over my career and it happened at all of them. So, copper fleas really do exist people.

I can't state it enough that I really loved my job. My self-esteem had been beaten down so badly that I did not think that I could ever do any kind of high-tech work, yet here I was. Having an awesome job made me feel happy but what made me even happier is that I also had lots of friends.

From the moment we arrived in Massachusetts, I blossomed, it was if I had shed a cloak of invisibility, people noticed me and actually wanted to be friends with me. Even though I had switched jobs my friendships that I had made in my other workplaces stayed intact and for the first time in my life I had a social life; shopping, BINGO, going out to eat or just hanging out and playing games, it was wonderful.

Socially I was fulfilled but spiritually I had yet to find someone to discuss all the metaphysical subjects I was so interested in. By chance one day at work helping a co-worker at a task we began talking and glory of glories she too was a psyki-do-dah like me. (Psyki-do-dah is a term I created many years ago in reference to anything metaphysical.)

Third memory: Double trouble. This is a collection of memories that I recall about my psyki-do-dah co-worker. My friend Teri had a young son who was very gifted. She told me he had only air signs in his zodiac and that she made him carry rocks and touch earth to try and ground him. Teri told me that while her son was still in the crib he would levitate his toys and stuffed animals from across the room into the crib with him. As he got older she had to keep an eye on him extra close in the bathtub because he would levitate the bubble bath and shampoo down to himself to make more bubbles. Teri also related that her son could read minds and that she had to reprimand him for doing it and tell him it was an invasion of privacy.

I shared books with her I had about the Indigo Children in an effort to help her understand his uniqueness. We talked about many subjects and like usual when I got energized and excited about something along comes wind and spikes in energy.

It took us awhile to figure it out, but we soon noticed that our combined energies played havoc with all the electronic equipment we worked with. Whenever we worked in the same room, bulbs would blow, machines would go wonky and nothing would get done until maintenance arrived.

Once we had figured out what was happening we went to our group leader Kay and told her why we are having so much down time. We told Kay that we couldn't work in the same room together especially on the same machine if we were to get any product out.

Now, this is a person with absolutely no spiritual leanings what so ever, who basically told us we were talking out our respective asses. I suggested we run a few experiments by having us work in the same room and in different rooms.

It did not take long to make a believer out of her for the first time she put us together after a separation the bulbs blew in 2 exposing units and the photo film coating machine went haywire spewing out film until the motor died, the whole room was down for almost the entire shift. From that day forward, we worked in separate rooms and our group leader did not ever want to test the theory again.

I had only worked at this company less than a year when it closed, it just wasn't equipped to handle the quick changing technology. The department I worked in was one of the first to grind to a halt as we were the ones who initiated the beginning process of building a circuit board. I hopped about helping in other departments until they too wound down. One of the jobs at this company that I was assigned to do in those final months will always remain in my mind.

Fourth memory: The barrels. Trying to make any possible profit they could get from their boards, management (or I should say my manager) tried to rectify a mistake on a large, expensive order of circuit boards.

The final stage in our type of shop was applying (by silk screening) a white legend onto the boards of words and numbers so the people who did the next process of adding components would know where to put them.

This lot of boards had been mistakenly legend and the ink was already cured. Because the boards were a high profit job and to save his own ass for the mistake, the manager in question decided to try and strip off the ink.

The manager who came up with this mad scheme was more than just a little bit of a chauvinist and if he could find a shitty job for a woman to do he found it. Unfortunately for me I was elected to be the one to try and salvage the mistakenly legend boards.

The manager escorted me to the lowest basement level where there wasn't even any floor, just dirt. The ceiling was low and stretching back into the darkness along the walls were barrels of chemicals, some new and some spent.

At the bottom of the steps was a platform made of pallets with two barrels setting there that had grounding wires attached to them, so they would not ignite from a spark. Handing me a rubber apron and a pair of rubber gloves he instructed me to soak the circuit boards in the barrels full of chemicals and scrub them of the legend, pointing at a scrub brush laying there; without another word he turned back up the steps leaving me alone in the barely lit dungeon full of chemicals.

The chemicals burned my eyes and seared my lungs, but I kept on scrubbing, my victim mindset making me obey any man in authority.

I had been at my task for a couple of hours when I heard footsteps and appearing in the dim glow of the single light bulb lighting the stairs was my group leader Kay. To say she was a bit put out at the sight of the job I had been given to do is an understatement. Mouthing a litany of obscenities and declaring where our manager could shove his boards, I was rescued from Dracula's basement.

Kay was a "take no shit, take charge" sort of person and everyone even upper management respected and quite possibly feared her a bit. From the beginning of our friendship she had appointed herself my guardian (as if she sensed the scared child within) even though she was five years my junior.

Upon returning to the land of the living, the main work level, I was sent to get cleaned up and I saw Kay through the window of the manager's office ripping him a new one in front of his boss.

There were no more trips for me down to the dungeon. I went on to assist in other departments under the glaring eye of my manager who presumed that I had whined to my friend about the job he had given me. For the remainder of my time at that company I could feel his wrath towards me searing into my every time I passed by him, it was a tangible, liquid feeling of hatred.

Fifth memory: The Fairy. I spent the remaining weeks/months working in the drill department, where you guessed it, holes were drilled in the panels for the future placement of wires and conductors. I worked with a woman, (I'll call her Willow) in the drilling department. Willow was only a few years older than me petite, slender to a point you wouldn't think she could survive a strong breeze.

I have already mentioned that at an early age I could see auras and feel energies from people, but when I met her I saw beyond the physical being and saw her soul, her true self.

There are dimensions to our world where magical beings live, co-existing alongside us humans in relative obscurity. The brief glimpses of these beings in their parallel existence next to ours are the basis of our fairytales, folklore and the prickly goosebumps on our arms when we catch something out of the corner of our eye or have the sensation of being watched.

Throughout history lucky people of high vibration and open mind have born witness to the Fey realm of Fairies, Pixies, Elementals, Unicorns, Sasquatch, etc. Like humans, their souls also travel the path of life, death and rebirth/reincarnation.

When I met Willow, another of my gifts emerged, the ability to see the home origin of a soul. Willow was a fairy soul that had reincarnated into the human dimension. I have had many, many encounters since then with other souls that have incarnated into the earthly plane from other dimensions and planets, but she was my first.

Three-dimensional Earth energy is very dense, and my friends Fairy soul, used to the lighter fourth dimension vibration had a difficult time existing in a human body, she was plagued by numerous allergies and had cancer needing both breasts removed. No matter the pain or irritations Willow suffered, she greeted each day with a smile with her joyous heart shining from her eyes. Like a butterfly she left a delicate footprint upon the earth before she faded away.

CHAPTER 14

❖

The Voice of No Reason

When my job finally came to an end with the closing of the business I did not immediately jump back into working at another factory. Even in my twenties I had back and leg issues and had been recently diagnosed with Degenerative Disc Disease.

I opted to work part-time for a while and got hired as a private cook at a Catholic rectory. There were several priests in residence a housekeeper and secretary. The main meal of the day was taken early afternoon as there were too many committees, programs, etc. to allow for a formal dinner time.

This was a wonderful job, like cooking for your family, I not only prepared the meal but sat down and ate it with them. The most interesting fact being that I wasn't even a Catholic. The conversations were varied and at times intense, the rule firmly adhered to, "what you hear or say here, stays here."

Along with new employment my husband and I moved into a new apartment, a duplex with the landlady living downstairs. My friend Kay also moved in with us.

My husband and I both loved to remodel and renovate homes and for a discount on our rent we agreed to strip the hardwood floors upstairs and down for our landlady. OMG, what a mess. The floors had been covered with the old linoleum that had a black tar like adhesive on the back and it had leeched into the wood. Days, no weeks it took to soak all that stickiness off before we could sand and polyurethane the wood but the final result was beautiful.

First memory: The revelation. Happy as I was in my marriage, sometimes things just felt off. We genuinely cared for each other, had common interests and a lackluster though regular sex life. Intimacy was only on Sundays and holidays. I remember kidding him on the approach of our first anniversary, it was a Sunday check 1. It was our anniversary check 2. It was his birthday check 3. And it was Valentine's day check 4. I told him he better eat his Wheaties!

I was putting laundry away and decided to straighten his dresser drawers and I found, buried beneath his clothes, homosexual literature. When Tim came home, I confronted him and he admitted to being gay.

I can't say that I was shocked for I remembered some gossip I had heard about him possibly being gay way back before we ever lived together. I was not even upset because I knew that he genuinely loved me, I was only concerned about any relationships he may have had and the health risks. The 80's were rampant with headlines and TV shows about HIV and Aids.

Truthfully, I felt relieved. I had thought that there was something wrong with me that he was not more sexually attracted to me, that it was somehow my fault, that I was flawed. My self-esteem as always in the negative. We discussed options, and both agreed that we wanted to stay together, after all we were 6 years into a happy marriage, sex aside.

There was another couple that we were very good friends with and we spent much of our free time at one another's houses doing the dinner and cards thing. They were a gay and straight couple with a child. We knew about them, but they did not know my husband was gay until after I had found out.

We got together with them and shared our similar situation and asked how they made it work. Since our respective spouses were both, "clean" we arranged that the men could get together to satisfy whatever yearnings they had thus preventing any forays into an un-safe environment. They were already friends and secretly attracted to each other, so the situation worked for all. The other wife and I did not ask for details, there was no kinky, exploitive four-way sexual drama playing out between us, the situation was dignified and private as we each truly loved our spouses.

In the small rural community where I came from homosexuality wasn't exactly a subject that came up often and was whispered about and fingers pointed behind closed doors. But I wasn't like the small minded, bigoted people I grew up around, I accepted people for who they were and my theory is that GOD, doesn't make mistakes and if he created people that loved their own gender then there was a reason and a lesson behind it.

I did not know then and still do not completely understand all the dynamics that go into our choices for coming into physical life, but I knew enough then that we are all unique to our purpose here on earth and that tolerance and love were key to our lessons.

When I found out about my husband's homosexuality it also, to my mind, clarified why he became an alcoholic. All those years of confusion and secrecy led him to drown his emotions in alcohol.

We had gone through a brief bout of Tim falling off the wagon shortly before we were married. I confronted him saying I wasn't stupid and knew he was drinking again, that I had found the bottles he had hidden, and he couldn't hide it from me. I told him he could choose a good life with me or the bottle, not both.

Tim sat there quietly for a moment then said, "I'll be right back" and went out to the barn where he had 2 bottles hidden that I did not know about.

I watched as he opened each bottle and poured it down the drain, he never drank again the whole time we were married and remained sober for at least 26 years that I know of.

Second memory: The bear. I was good friends with my landlady, we were BINGO buddies. In fact. I can't remember if I met her at BINGO or met her the first time we came to see the apartment, either way we spent a lot of time together.

She had a lot of health issues and had to spend much time in bed so her son lived with her to help out. He worked but drank quite a bit and I'm pretty sure he helped himself to his mother's meds.

My husband worked second shift and got home about 11:30 and immediately upon getting home would hop in the shower as he worked with lots of chemicals. One night as my husband came into the bedroom from his shower we were discussing his day when we heard this moaning growling sound like a bear, coming from the front room.

We listened and heard it again. Kay was asleep in the bedroom next door so I got her up and we all crept into the living room to investigate armed with a crowbar or a bat I can't remember which. We flick the light switch on and there curled up on my loveseat, "bear" naked was our landlady's son. Drunk as a skunk, as the saying goes.

My husband yelled his name and told him to go downstairs he was in the wrong apartment. (They used to live upstairs until our landlady's back got too bad.) No response. By this time, I was full on pissed off and using my, "mean mom voice" yelled his name, saying "you're in the wrong apartment get your naked ass off my loveseat and get back downstairs!"

He shot up like a firecracker had been shoved up his butt, and kept repeating, "I'm sorry I apologize."

He was so stoned he couldn't even open his eyes all the way, my husband handed him a robe and off he went. Having been raised by his mother, a strong-willed woman, he had instinctively responded to the tone of my voice.

You might be wondering why this memory stands out for me and why I chose to share it. 1: it's funny and 2: it's the first time I stood up to a man. I stepped forward and took care of the situation myself. I did not wait for my husband or strong-willed friend to handle the problem. Small and brief as the incident was it was a HUGE step in my developing esteem as a woman.

My husband and Kay looked at me in astonishment as I usually shrank into the background when faced with any conflict. If I he had challenged me I don't think I would have been so confident, for even today 34 years later I get chest pains and back away if provoked to argue or if someone yells at me…. baby steps.

Third memory. The voice. Not long after the incident of the "bear" I was puttering in the kitchen and heard a clear and distinct voice in my head say, "you have to move back to home."

I stopped what I was doing and just stood still and analyzed what had just happened. I not only heard the words in my head, I saw them, felt them and knew without question that I needed to heed them. I did not even question why.

When my husband came home from work that night I told him what had happened and he did not question it either. The very next day we started making plans to move. My memory fails me a bit here, I know we agreed I would move first and take the car. My husband would stay with someone and continue working until I got everything situated back home.

I don't remember where he went or who he stayed with. My friend also had to find another place to live and my quick decision put a momentary wrinkle in our relationship.

I did not dwell on the reason or lack thereof for my moving, I just set in motion all the things I needed to do to accomplish it. I knew we could go back to my in-law's country house to live as it was vacant and that I could stay at my parents' house until I had a job lined up and money for the turning on of utilities and such.

Three weeks after arriving back home, my mother had to have surgery and I had to care for her again, the reason orchestrated by Spirit for my hasty move. Only a few weeks after finally getting settled back in the farm house and starting work I got a call from my mother-in-law that they had to sell the property do to her ill health and need to go on Medicare, so before my husband could even join me, I had to move back to Massachusetts.

Over the next five years we would move back and forth between Massachusetts and home several more times, each time prompted by the, "voice of no reason" the purpose for the moves never becoming apparent until three weeks or three months, always a three.

I was told to move back home but also back to Massachusetts, the reasons all different, me taking care of my mom, my mom taking care of me, to meet someone that helped me spiritually, or me help them. Not once did I question the message even though it was a huge financial burden to move so frequently, it seemed like as soon as we recovered from one move there was another.

I took a lot of flak from family and friends for (from their viewpoint) my gypsy ways. I did not try and validate my reason to anyone, I just followed where Spirit dictated. It was not easy, it takes 6 months to recuperate from a move financially not to mention the stress of finding employment and the physical strain of packing, lugging and lifting. Spirit always provided enough means for me to go where it dictated.

In our last move as a married couple we again came back home and rented an apartment over a store. The building was old dating from the mid 1800's. There had been no renovations done to the apartment in nearly 20 years. The modern renovations were minimal at best and there was much evidence of the apartment's roots in the previous century.

We did our usual makeover and stripped layers of wallpaper and paint to bring new life to the space. There were several ghosts in residence making their presence known to us both as my husband was also intuitive. (He had to be in order to live with me and my voice!) Our cats were also aware of the ghosts, staring off into odd corners and pausing before entering rooms and snorting or giving a low growl.

Fourth memory: A step back in time. We had the main rooms all finished leaving only the two spare bedrooms to be stripped and redone. I chose to start the smaller of the two rooms first and from the moment I peeled the first strip of wallpaper off, I became obsessed with finishing the room.

I was like a woman possessed, I couldn't stop, I barely slept, barely ate, only leaving the apartment if I had to go to work. Finally, with two days off, I finished, having worked round the clock. It was completely finished right down to the placement of furniture.

Placing the last piece of furniture, I shook my head, blinked my eyes and truly saw the room for the first time. I had done the room in a total Victorian theme. The wallpaper and paint in shades of dark green, burgundy, dusty rose with hints of gold. The furnishings, knick-knacks, and artwork all Victorian, the drapes heavy and fringed pulled back with a lace panel behind them.

I started to hear a whispering and called my husband into the room to see if he could hear it too. We could not see anything but we heard the voice of a little girl telling us that it had been her room in days gone by and that she had died from eating green grapes. She told us that the love, joy and light we put into the remodeling of the apartment was the incentive that caused her to encourage me to redo her room. She told us that after her death only sadness and indifference had ever lived there.

Our little ghost thanked us and told us that she was ready to go now that she had found someone to bring the love back to her home. We never heard from her again and I never remodeled the remaining room. It was as if I had used everything I had to bring her room back to her.

We did not get anymore information about the green grapes. Did she choke on a green grape, eat an unripe fruit or a poison berry that looked like a grape? In the long run it did not matter, what mattered was that the little ghost girl left the earthly plane with a smile on her face.

My husband and I had been in the apartment for 2 years when we decided to end our marriage. We both had grown in confidence over the course of our marriage and were ready to embark on different paths.

I felt I wanted a man who was completely mine not someone who found the opposite sex more attractive. I wanted someone to love me 100 percent not as much as he could. Even more than that I wanted to be in a smoke free environment. My husband was a 2 or 3 pack a day smoker. My parents had been smokers. I had over the last year developed an intense hatred of cigarettes.

I had been warned my whole life not to smoke or be around chemicals because of the scaring in my lungs from the earlier poisoning. In reality I had probably inhaled more second-hand smoke than if I had taken up smoking.

I can honestly say that in the 10 years of our marriage we had never had a fight. That is not to say we did not have disagreements we did, but there was no yelling or shouting, we really were the best of friends.

We planned our divorce very civilly. I decided to move back to Massachusetts where job opportunities were better and I had a lot of friends there for support. We went through our things and I picked and chose what I wanted to keep and they were set aside for me. My husband even went so far as to bring home a flyer from the company store where he worked for me to pick out a new set of dishes that he would pay for and get me.

With hugs and best wishes I moved back up north with only some clothes, Tim to bring my things to me once I had found a place to live.

The saddest was parting from my kitties. It was decided that he would keep the cats as we did not know how long it would take me to get settled or if I would even be able to find a place where I could have a cat.

I wish all divorces could be as amicable as ours was especially where children are concerned. A little respect goes a long way and seems to have gone out of fashion these days. I could have been hateful about his being gay, furious about his omission from the beginning. But I could not feel that way. I really loved him as a person and we were both wounded people.

Neither one of us was whole, each of us missing parts of ourselves from the circumstances of our younger lives. Like a puzzle our gaps and angles fit together supporting each other until we had filled in those spaces with our own personal growth and as the gaps filled we slowly pulled apart each of us whole.

CHAPTER 15

Clueless

I stayed with my friend Mary when I first returned to Massachusetts. We had worked together at a couple of different factories and we were also BINGO buddies. I got hired where my friend Kay was working and she again became my group leader.

Within a few weeks I had found an apartment and my ex-husband some of his friends brought my furnishings up to me. Except for a couple of months in my first apartment I had never lived all by myself. I was completely at ease being on my own but had absolutely no clue about how to go about the dating thing.

First memory: Singles dance. One of the nicer hotels in the area hosted a singles dance. I can't remember if it was weekly or monthly, so I bit the bullet and decided to go to one. I bought a new outfit had my hair done and off I went.

Nervous and scared I entered the reception hall of the hotel where the dance was being held. I felt like I had when standing in the hallway of my high school not knowing what to do or where to go, feeling a panic attack on the horizon.

I got a drink and sat at a table, taking a sip I watched the couples on the dance floor. I am one of only a few not dancing and the only one not in a small group talking. I felt my aloneness sticking out like a sore thumb. I sit there through several songs watching as some couples danced again with the same partner and saw the men ask other women to dance. I notice I am the only woman who has not been asked.

After sitting through several rounds of songs the DJ announces that the next dance, after the break, will be the lady's choice, the ladies able to ask the man. I tell myself I can do this and get up, introduce myself and ask a guy to dance. He said no. I ask another, he said no. My fragile self can take no more and I leave.

Feeling a loser, I put thoughts of dating out of my mind for the moment. I worked, spent some time with friends and walked around the city a lot. I worked second shift, so when I got up in the morning I would walk downtown and just window shop. My car had broken down and I was saving every penny for bills and repairs.

I decided once again to try the singles dance and this time I had a nice guy ask me to dance. We talked and danced the rest of the evening and he asked me out on a date. My first date at age 32, we went to the movies.

Afterwards we came back to my place for drinks and next thing I knew we were in bed having sex. It was all I knew how to do, just let it happen. I said something to him about it being the first time I had been with someone since my divorce and mid stroke he stops and starts crying.

He went on to tell me that I too was his first and that his divorce happened because his wife had a miscarriage and could not face the reality or him. All this as he was poised above me his tears dripping on my chest. Shaking his head and gathering himself together he said, "I started this I can finish."

I said, "no" and "goodbye"

The whole experience made me feel more horrible than I had in years, wrong for me, wrong for him, just plain wrong on so many levels.

Second memory: Is that really me. I was visiting my friend Kay one day when I remarked on a pair of jeans she had, saying how much I liked them. Kay told me to try them on, my response being, "they won't fit me I'm too fat"

Kay persisted, so I grudgingly tried them on and they fit! I was totally shocked. I had been so focused on figuring out how to proceed as a single woman that I had not noticed how my aimless wandering around town had changed my body. I had lost 50 pounds. Kay gave me the pants and took me shopping for some new clothes.

That pair of jeans was the impetus for a whole new mindset for me. For the first time in my life I felt attractive. I was not skinny by any means but I was comfortable with myself, it was the first time that I realized that what I thought about me is what I reflected out to the world and what they world saw.

My new self-image made me more approachable to men as friends and as flirtations. I engaged in flirtation with several men and when they hinted at wanting more, I would walk away. Me, the human equivalent of a door mat, for the first time in my life walked away from sexual encounters.

Third memory: Big mistake. I finally ended up in a relationship with a guy from work who I was not really attracted to but he was really interested in me. My new-found confidence not strong enough to hold out for the gold but to settle for what was offered.

We spent a lot of time together and within 2 months he moved in with me. Shortly after moving in with me he lost his job at our mutual workplace and he found a new job, on day shift, while I worked second shift.

Our separation during work hours did not go well. I had not noticed how possessive he was as we had spent so much time together but his true colors quickly became apparent. He became verbally abusive and would get mad if I spent time with my girlfriends, threatening violence. In public he always had to hold my hand to show ownership of me.

We had gone out to dinner with my friend Kay and her boyfriend and even at dinner he had to hold my hand under the table. The guys were talking about some girl that they thought they both may have mutually known and Kay and I just to be smart asses started talking about a fake guy and when describing him. Angered at my discussing another man my boyfriend started squeezing my hand real hard. My fingers hurt so bad that I thought he might have broken some. I know tears started in my eyes and I excused myself to go to the rest room. Being gone a bit long, Kay came into the restroom looking for me and I told her what had happened. Of course, her first instinct was to go out into the restaurant and beat the crap out of him.

I talked Kay out of making a scene and we made plans for her to come over one day after my boyfriend went to work. I don't know if I was more scared or pissed off that my boyfriend had become a live-in stalker.

My boyfriend would call me on his morning break to question me, wanting to know if I had gone out anywhere, what was I wearing to work, did it show any cleavage, telling me not to wear make-up. When Kay came over, we talked about all this and she informed me that she had found out through friends at work that he had people at our job site spying on me for him, telling him if I talked to any guys and if so, how long.

I had talked to my mom earlier that day and she told me that when the four of us, me and my boyfriend and Kay and her boyfriend had come to visit her a few weeks earlier to visit her she had a vision of my boyfriend keeping me captive in a room when she shook his hand. This bit of information had my "creeper" meter running on screech.

I knew then that I had to get out and it had to be in secret. I called my mother back after talking to Kay and had her get me a PO box so I had somewhere to forward my bills. I called my utility companies and scheduled a shut off date with instructions on how important it was that my forwarding address not be given out.

I talked to my manager at work and gave him my notice, I told him the reason and that he could not let anyone know except upper management because of the people my boyfriend had spying on me. I really felt it was a matter of life and death and stressed that to him.

On the day planned for my escape (for that's what it was) I pretended to be asleep until I heard my boyfriends' car leave then I jumped out of bed. I had been secretly packing a few things and had bags hidden in the back of the closet. My friend Kay came over for moral support but could not help me as she had just had knee surgery.

I answered my boyfriends' break time phone call, my voice giving no hint of my plans. I knew I had to have my car packed and be gone before noon as sometimes he surprised me by coming home at lunch to check on me and approve or disapprove my outfit for the day.

Guilt still a big component to my makeup I left him a note telling him I was sorry that I did not care for him as he cared for me and he deserved to find someone who would love him. I explained that I had scheduled the utility shut off to give him enough time to get them switched into his name if he chose to stay there and wished him well.

I packed what I could fit into my car and walked away from the rest, many of my beloved kitchen items, my antiques, knick-knacks and artwork a fitting sacrifice for my freedom and life. My car, newly fixed and not really up to the trip, left me praying the whole way to make it home.

I guess I should have been a little more specific in my prayer, for when I got off the interstate and stopped for gas only one hour from home, my car died, never to be resurrected again. I called my mother who came and got me and a few necessities and we had the car towed a few days later.

The garage that took the car called me some days later and exclaimed that they could not believe that the car had actually made the trip. The engine in the car, which had been replaced in Massachusetts, wasn't even the right size or model for the car, the engine mounts didn't even line up. The engine not securely attached and the way everything was hooked up the car shouldn't have run, they told me it was a miracle it didn't fall out on the trip. I think I have very good and attentive Angels.

I walked into my childhood home to the ringing of the telephone, my mom answered, it was him. My mom played stupid and concerned, stating she did not know where I was and had not heard from me.

Unknown to me my boyfriend, had either copied or memorized every number in my address book. I called my friend Kay and she told me she had been his first phone call and that he was insane with anger, informing her that, "if Sophie left me for another man, I'm going to kill him and her too!"

For nearly 2 years I could not answer the phone at my parents' house. There were numerous calls from him and he would also get other people to call for him saying they were friends of mine from. These anonymous people would never give their name, a heads up to my mother of who it really was as all my friends knew my mother and would have talked to her.

CHAPTER 16

Limbo

I was not thrilled about living under my parents' roof again but throughout my life I had learned there is a reason and purpose behind everything. I had suffered for years with a strange abdominal pain that would take me suddenly with no warning. I would be walking along when mid-step it would feel like someone shoved a knife up my vagina and simultaneously jabbed one in at the top of my uterus and twisted each.

The pain would be so severe that I would just drop to the floor. I had it happen at home, at work, while shopping at a store and out walking. At least twice being rushed to the ER where after finally being seen the pain would have abated and they found nothing conclusive.

First memory: Surgery. I had only been back home a couple of weeks when I went out for a walk with my next-door neighbor, we were only about a quarter mile from the house when one of those stabbing pains hit and I dropped to the ground with a scream. I lay there crying for a few moments before I was able to get up with the help of my neighbor. Making it to a house we called my mother and she came and got me with the car.

Sitting was impossible it felt like I was sitting on the knife and each rock in the road felt like I was riding over a boulder and sheer torture. It was bearable if I lay on my side in the back seat but still cried out at each bump. For the first time the pain had not abated by the time a physician saw me in the ER and he was able to observe just how much pain I really experienced in these episodes. I believe I had an ultra-sound that day which showed ovarian cysts.

The head gynecological surgeon was on call that day and he came to see me and surgery was scheduled. Within days I had surgery and three quarters of my left ovary was taken too covered in cysts to be saved and a large cyst was taken from my right ovary. After recovery the doctor came and told me what he had found and in addition to the cysts removed he told me that there was unusual scarring in my fallopian tubes. Odd, because that kind of scarring usually only occurs after surgery. He Informed me that he had removed as much of the scar tissue from my tubes as he could but the finger like appendages at the end of the tubes were now more like stubs.

The doctor also informed me that my chances of getting pregnant before surgery would have been impossible but there was some slight chance now after the surgery with some help. I never had the stabbing pain again but did suffer progressively from severe menstrual pain as I got older.

I talked of my missing pregnancies earlier and of the physical exam on the spaceship, could the unusual scarring in my fallopian tubes have been a result of that earlier probing? I did not think of this at the time of the surgery, not until the day I wrote this. All I thought of at that time was that now I had a chance to get pregnant, slim as it was, and no husband.

My mother had won a trip as part of a promotion for the opening of a new business in a neighboring town and gave the ticket for 2 to me and I asked my friend Kay to come down and go with me. So off I went to Ft. Lauderdale and Grand Bahama, to recuperate in the sun. My one and only trip out of the United states, so far.

After recovering from my surgery, I got hired at the company where my dad worked on a temporary program and thankfully not on the same shift as him. My previous experience in the circuit board shops enabling me to get a position in a little more high-tech area, not too strenuous or too hot. The day I had just enough money to get my own place I moved out.

I found a one-bedroom apartment only a few blocks from the plant so I could walk to work having no car. I was also able to walk to shops and restaurants easily. Settled in my new place my focus became finding a mate. I said mate, not husband. I really did not care if I was married I just wanted a baby.

Second memory: What goes around, comes around. A friend of mine set me up with a guy he had met at an AA meeting. I couldn't seem to break away from getting into a relationship with someone in recovery. First my ex-husband and then my live-in boyfriend (also a recovering alcoholic and drug user) I seemed destined to draw these men to me. I think the fact that I did not really drink and would rather cut my wrists than do any kind of drugs made me a safe harbor for these men.

It's funny, but I can't even remember the guy's name now but we dated for several months. Feeling that we were getting fairly close in our relationship I offered him a key to my apartment. Arriving home one day after work I found the key and a note on my kitchen counter. In the note he explained how in his years of drug addiction he had been with a woman who like my former boyfriend had been possessive and controlling and he still carried that fear with him. He apologized and said he was not emotionally ready for a serious relationship.

It was only now as I was writing about this relationship that I recognized that I had been given the opportunity to view both sides of my own situation, having left someone and myself being left by someone. I had left my former boyfriend a kind but final note and I, had been left a kind but final note.

I believe this is the quickest karmic turn around I have ever seen. Do I have more of them in my life that I haven't recognized? I don't know, but I will examine the events of my life more closely from now on.

I went out a few times with other men but I hated the bars almost as much as I hated cigarettes. Whatever I was looking for in a man it was not here. My life for the first time had become mundane, go to work, come home. I did not want a repeat of any of the drama that I had encountered my whole life but I did want friends. I really only had one close friend nearby and she was busy with working and family.

My mom would come get me for the day on the weekends to visit at home and I noticed that without us kids to bully dad had resorted to emotionally abusing my mother. He would put her down and call he up to 20 times a day to nag her about something.

Dad was also flagrant in his extramarital affairs and my mom's retaliation was to spend his money. I asked why she didn't leave him and her response was, "I love this house, I love this land, its mine and only death can make me leave it."

I talked to my friend Kay and asked her if she had seen anything of my old boyfriend and if she knew if he was still looking for me. Kay told me it had been awhile since he had been around any of my friends asking my whereabouts. I decided that I did not want to live in fear of him anymore. I wanted my friends, a social life and a full-time job with benefits.

I felt I was existing in a state of limbo, my life that had been interrupted by my misalliance with the wrong man and waiting to be resumed. When my part-time contract was up at my job I moved back to New England. I still had no car so I'm assuming Kay came and got me, my memory still playing tricks on me.

CHAPTER 17

Power

I was able to get back into the circuit board shop where I had been working when I had to flee so abruptly. I got hired to the same shift as Kay (third) and she was again to be my group leader. Along with working together Kay and I also rented a house with another of her friends, 2 cats and a dog. The 3 of us sharing expenses and chores.

My Initial interview, paperwork and tour of my new work area (I would now be working a different department than I had before) had to be done on first shift early in the morning so I could meet with the third shift supervisor.

First memory: What the heck! The department supervisor had escorted me down the hall and through the swinging doors into the work area. I am slightly behind the supervisor and I know he is talking to me above the sound of running machinery. As the door swings shut behind me I am looking out across the open room to my right and I lock gazes with a man.

I froze, I could not move, a myriad of emotions running through my body as I stared into the most captivating eyes I had ever seen. (The rest of the package pretty sweet too) It took me a moment to realize that I indeed had frozen, that is my etherical self, had frozen, my physical body was at least four steps ahead of me still following the supervisor.

Entranced, I had literally stepped out of my body, Why? How? And most importantly who was that gorgeous hunk! I know this episode occurred in only a split second but my mind was able to process it all in that time period. In less time than it takes to blink I am back in my body and following the supervisor grudgingly, not wanting to break that gaze. Reluctantly I turned my head but not before I noticed the gorgeous guy leaning as far back as he could on his perch to watch me pass out of sight. I do believe some mutual appreciation was going on there.

I really loved the work I did and was the best at what I did the only one to match me and do better than me was Kay. I became the official trainer whenever we had new hires. I determined early on that I would treat and teach people the exact opposite way that dad had taught me.

I was kind, patient and did not overload the new hire with too much information all at once. One of the first things I always told anyone I was training is, "there is no such thing as a stupid question, the only stupid question is the question never asked, questions let me know you are curious and wanting to learn your job."

For the most part the people I worked with daily were like family, but there are always a few in any work environment who carry enormous chips on their shoulders and are consumed by petty jealousies. Some few, were jealous of my work output, but it did not bother me.

I have never been one to enjoy or feel compelled to any form of competition with another human being. I only ever compete with myself, striving always to do the best that I can do. My emotional abuse had been directed at my shortcomings: you're stupid, you're worthless not you're more stupid than so and so. I was never compared to another so I never tried to out do or compete with anyone. My mental conditioning making me my own worst enemy and biggest critic.

Second memory: The kiss: The man of my infatuation worked on first shift so the only time I could see him was the half hour overlap of our shifts. I made numerous excuses to walk in and out of the area to ogle him, nod and say hello. I was still shy about approaching a man and cautious now because the last man I had a relationship with at that company was still stalking me.

One day hanging out in the hallway with Kay, in front of the time clock, waiting to punch out, the man of my dreams stopped to chat with Kay and me. He told me I looked nice and said we should get together sometime. I stood there blushing and stammering and Kay, unafraid of anything or anyone and to tease me, because she knew I had the hots for him, leaned over to him and said, "you should hook up with her because she can suck a golf ball through a garden hose!"

I thought I would die right there on the spot, wishing the floor would open up and swallow me whole. I couldn't believe Kay would say such a thing. I could feel the blush reaching all the way to my toes.

His eyes popped, he laughed and taking me by the arm said, "come here with me for a minute."

He guided me across the hall and through a doorway that was a stairwell for access to the second floor. Spinning me around he put his arms around me pushed me against the wall and proceeded to kiss me senseless.

Senseless isn't the word to describe that kiss for every sense in my body and extending into my auric field was alive with sensation. I had never known true passion until that moment and I was in awe of it. Releasing me he asked me for a phone number to call and told me he would call me that afternoon before I went to bed.

I was a nervous wreck waiting for that phone call which eventually came that day. We made plans to get together that weekend and we made no pretense that it was for any other reason than to have sex.

Third memory: Power. Our first time together was explosive to say the least. We were like an addiction that could not be satisfied, a craving that you could not appease, wanting more. I was not to become a victim to it though, after that first time I called the shots, the where and the when.

For the first time in my life I did not feel powerless in regard to sex. In fact, I felt the exact opposite. I felt powerful. I was an avid reader and historical novels and biographies one of my favorite genres. I had read numerous accounts of wars having been fought and kingdoms lost and won over the obsession of a woman.

I had been an unwilling participant in the lust that drove men first hand, but I had never experienced or expressed the flip side of a woman's passion. Women have throughout history, been unfavorably depicted in regard to sex. They have been portrayed as victims: rape, forced into unwanted marriage or prostitution. If a woman showed strength and owned her sexuality and used it to get what she wanted from men she was considered: evil, unnatural, a whore.

Even though I had admired these strong women I had read about I could not understand how they wielded such power. I was so far removed from them on the opposite end of the spectrum. The fact that I, myself, could command, even a small bit of that power and confidence was huge.

It is no coincidence that as I am writing about this subject my husband turned on the tv and an old movie is playing about a woman being sent to an asylum because she refused to be a paramour to one of the aristocracies. This is validation for me that I am on the right path and speaking my truth, for there are really no coincidences.

Coincidences are orchestrated by us, before even coming into life. They are part of our plan/blueprint to achieving our life lessons, popping up throughout our life as reminders that we are on the right path and that we are not alone on our journey.

Passion, lust, infatuation, essentially sex has been one of the main fuels powering the machine of war throughout history. The only thing greater is greed, and then that is often referenced to sexually, as in, "the LUST for power compelled him"

Humans are oriented to sex and power as is all life. It is what makes up our basic survival instinct. Unfortunately, the human evolution from this primal survival instinct to that of a more spiritual state of being has been retarded in some way. Our spiritual growth is stuck in the heavy, third dimensional, survival vibration.

This stagnation of our spiritual progress has caused an imbalance in our sex, survival, power and pleasure centers creating the current explosion of sex crimes, sex trafficking, drug addiction and gambling. The lust for power and pleasure has become epidemic.

Wow, not sure where that just came from, I believe you have just born witness to a spontaneous channeling.

I exercised my new sexual prowess maybe a little too much, I found out I was very good at being bad. The poor guy didn't stand a chance I used my lust and imagination to keep him enthralled, he never knew what to expect.

We were a couple of weeks into our sexual tango before I even knew that he was still married and living with his wife. I felt a momentary wrinkle of guilt but it did not stop me. I was still riding the high of the realization that sex could be fun, pleasurable and fulfilling on a level I had never experienced before.

At the core of my being the feelings of guilt, shame, fear, worthlessness were rooted in the sexual abuse of my childhood. I needed to be released from that. I had to embrace the sexual aspect of myself in all its nuances, the good, the bad and the ugly truth of it.

Do not think for a minute that my lover was an innocent in this affair, that I overpowered any resistance. My lover was a player and I was but one of a number of women to fall under the spell of his looks and charm. He even cheated on me with a friend of mine.

I tried to tell myself that I was in love with him even managing some weak tears over his betrayal, but deep inside I recognized it for what it was. It was a liberation for me from the negative chains of sexual slavery that had held me all my life.

My friends and I had been sharing our house for almost a year. All three of us being on third shift, made it easy to plan and do things together. The only time we actually slept at night was occasionally on the weekend if not working overtime.

Fourth memory: The bracelet. My roommates and I had planned on going out for brunch on our day off. I got up got dressed and noticed that my bracelet was missing. I had taken to wearing a bracelet my mother had given me, nothing expensive, but I liked it. The bracelet was gold hearts interspaced with little faux pearls. I had been wearing it continuously for about two weeks, even to bed.

I called Kay into my bedroom to help me move the bed away from the wall to see if it had come unclasped and fallen there having already checked the bedding and floor. No luck.

Kay and I discussed that maybe it had fallen off the day before and I had not noticed. We searched the downstairs and along the sidewalk on the way to the car. I gave the back seat a quick look before getting in but still no luck.

Resigned to the fact that I had lost my bracelet, I buckled up in the backseat and sat back. Kay had asked me a question but I had trouble understanding her so I unbuckled my seatbelt to lean forward and as I extended my left arm I felt something and low and behold my bracelet was on my wrist.

I jumped forward on my seat shoving my left arm to the front of the car so Kay could see my bracelet, shouting as I did so, "Oh my fucking word, LOOK!"

Kay nearly drove off the street as we both exclaimed over the bracelet's appearance. I know it was not just my imagination, we had just spent 10 minutes looking for it.

Why did it disappear?

Where did it go?

Why did it reappear?

No clue. I was so astonished. I think it happened to remind me of miracles, that they can happen at any time. I also believe it happened so I would bring some focus back to my spiritual self. My whole focus over the last year had been to work as many hours as I could and pursue my carnal interests.

Our year lease was up and me and my roommates decided to go our separate ways, boyfriends and work locations dictating where we went. So off I went, with my cat in one hand and my fledgling self confidence in the other.

CHAPTER 18

The Healing

When my roommates and I split-up I still did not have a vehicle, so I had to concentrate my efforts in finding an apartment near where my job was located that I could afford on my own.

With some effort I finally found an apartment in the neighboring town of the one where my place of employment was. The biggest drawback being the apartment was exactly 4 miles from my doorstep to the parking lot of work and I had to walk it.

I have mentioned throughout my tale that I suffered from back and leg issues. While still married, 3 years prior to our divorce, I had been hospitalized with a herniated disc. The hospital in question I believe, used me as a guinea pig to try a new medication. I think the drug was called Decadron. Anyway, the drug was supposed to shrink the swollen disc. For 10 days I was restricted to bed with an ever-decreasing dose of the medication given intravenously.

At the end of the 10 days the doctor came in and asked if I felt good enough to go home. With a fake smile pasted on my face and a nod of my head I said yes. My mother was there to take me home as my husband was working. I remember nearly passing out from the pain when getting in and out of the car.

Arriving at my house my mother got me settled on the couch and then proceeded to make me a pot of her fabulous vegetable beef soup which I was craving and had requested.

Ignoring doctor's orders not to do stairs and in abhorrence of having to use a bucket to go to the bathroom in for the next 2 weeks (our only bathroom upstairs) I went upstairs to my comfortable bed. Technically I did not walk up those stairs for by the time I got to the bottom step, my body was done and I crawled.

The treatment did not work and for the next 7 years I lived on Ibuprofen. I would have good days, bad days and ever increasingly horrible days with soul-sucking pain that begged me to end it all. By the time I moved into my new apartment in Massachusetts, I knew I needed to again seek professional help.

First memory. Back surgery. The repetitious movements, heavy lifting required at my job played enough havoc on my poor body but the move to my new apartment was the last straw that broke this camel's back. I had to use a cane to walk and my left leg had started to drag like that of a stroke victim.

Pain or not I still went to work. At times I was able to catch rides into work with coworkers, but when I couldn't, with cane in hand I walked the 4 miles dragging my leg, tears streaming down my face. Do or die was the precept I had been raised with, well I wasn't dead so I did. My willfulness adding insult to injury and exacerbating the nerve damage.

It did not take long for me to get an appointment with a neurosurgeon and for once in my life I had good health insurance that would actually pay for an MRI to be done. The doctor told me that in my case surgery would be best as there was too much damage to be corrected by therapy alone.

The surgery scheduled, my mother came up to be with me for the operation and to stay for my first week of recovery. The surgery took several hours and I spent 2 days in the hospital before going home. I immediately noticed a lessening of the pain and some improvement in the use of my leg.

After my mother left I had to take a taxi to my surgeon's office for check-ups and for removal of stitches, leaving me penniless in no time as my short-term disability had not come through. Eventually I ran out of food and had to call my brother and ask him if he could come down and buy me some groceries to last until my check came.

My brother said yes, though I think not too happily. It had been at least a year since I had seen him and things still were not comfortable between us. He took me to the grocery store and while standing in line, leaning on the cart for support, the lady behind me rammed me in the back with her cart. I remember pain so intense that I wanted to puke then nothingness.

I don't remember my brother bringing me home or how long I had disappeared for. It had been years since I had a blackout the only realization being that apparently severe enough pain could trigger one.

I still do not know anymore now, than I did then, or as a youth what happens to my conscience self during an episode. I remember being obsessed with the movie Sybil, after I had watched it and wondering if I had a split personality. I too had read the book, The Minds of Billy Milligan, also dealing with multiple personalities.

I never sensed another personality. I never had anyone question that I might not have been the same person, but I wondered. Frankly, a part of me wished to have a split personality, the idea seeming glamorous, unique or at least special.

In my youth I always felt, "different" but not in a good way. To me different meant ugly, slow, stupid, uncoordinated, unlovable. Now I think of my, "differentness" as unique, comprised of curiosity, humor, open mindedness, creativity and a determination not to be swayed by the status quo.

So, do I have a split or multiple personality? I think I do but not in the way you may think. I do not have another persona that answers to another name and pops out to take over when the host Anne is overwhelmed by something. I am a multiple of me.

When retreating into my secret garden I connect with universal energy and love, drinking it in like a tonic, healing my body and soul, until strengthened enough to return. I awaken as myself Sophie, stronger, able to cope, drawing upon the energies I have stored.

Several weeks into my convalescence I started physical therapy, it was a torturous experience. I was still in therapy when my sick leave ended and went back to work. I was not making much progress, barely able to do even a third of the exercises I should have been able to do by that point and my insurance would not cover the extra sessions needed.

I was in miserable pain at work, the therapy aggravating whatever relief I had obtained from the surgery. There was just so much damage. The nerve in question had been compressed for so long it was like an electrical cord that a heavy piece of furniture had been setting on for years occasionally letting a spark through to power whatever devise intermittently. It became to painful to work so I made the decision to quit my job and once again move back to Pennsylvania to give my body the time to heal.

I had kept contact and remained friends with my ex-husband, who with friends, drove up from PA to retrieve me and my furniture. I settled back into my parents' house and again to my mothers' care. My mother and I could not seem to end this dance of co-dependent nursing, me taking care of her and her then taking care of me, a seeming never ending square dance.

Second memory. Spiritual healing. My mothers' knees never really improved from her surgeries the absence of her kneecaps only creating another problem. Shortly before I returned home to convalesce from my back surgery, my mother had visited a local woman whom she had struck up a friendship with.

The woman was a spiritual medium who gave readings in person and over the phone. Visiting one day the lady told my mother that she had contact with a spiritual doctor that had never been in physical form that could do healings here in the physical world, going on to say she could arrange for the spiritual doctor to come to my mother and work on her knees.

My mother had to pick a time of day that she could be resting with her legs up and allow the doctor to do his work. The medium contacted the doctor and acting as an intermediary set up the time of day for the treatments to occur.

When I got home my mother excitedly told me about her spiritual healing treatments and I was able to observe them in person. At the appointed time my mother would kick back in her recliner and we three mom, dad and I watched in amazement as we observed tiny points of light moving around my mothers' knees. If what was being done started to get painful my mother would instantly fall asleep as if given anesthesia.

As my mothers' healing treatments continued, her agility increased, able to go up and down stairs in normal stride unlike she had been able to do for nearly 30 years. Mom had even stopped into show off her miraculous recovery to her orthopedic surgeon, smiling, twirling and breaking out in a polka for him. The surgeon laughed with her in congratulations and told her that whatever she was doing to keep up the good work.

As my mother improved before my eyes, my own healing progress had ground to a halt somewhere between, "will this never end and I wish I was dead." Days and nights were misery, no relief in either.

My mother took me one day to meet her friend the medium and asked if she could also set up a healing time with the spiritual healer for me. I told her the time of day (I picked 10 pm) I would make myself available for the healing to occur and within moments she had a confirmation.

That night I lay in bed and at the precise time I had chosen I felt the first zings of energy moving along my spine across my hip and down my leg. That first night the energy was mild more like an electric eye tracing the path of pain and disability.

As the days and weeks progressed the healing became more intense often accompanied by a voice in my head telling me to lie in a particular position or on my stomach. I would get jolts that felt like I was receiving chiropractic adjustments my body being pressed down on and then springing up from the bed several inches.

In the darkness of my room I could see multiple points of light working on my body and other lights off to the side as if observing in an operating theatre. Like my mother, if it became too painful, I would instantly fall asleep. Within days of the treatments I began improving.

Another thing that seemed to have improved was my dad's demeanor. Observing the healing being done on my mother had awakened an interest in metaphysical studies and related topics like earth changes in him. Dad had acquired more than a passing interest in these subjects and read and talked about them enthusiastically.

Forever wary on anything in which dad was concerned I had my own theory on why he was expressing gentleness, kindness and regard to humanity and Mother Earth. I thought it was out of fear.

Woven into and throughout esoteric teachings is the concept of karma, which its most basic meaning is, "what goes around comes around." If you're a bastard in this lifetime, you make up for it in the next. Dad had been a bastard and then some this time around and he feared the karmic backlash of that even hinting at it a time or two.

Was dad really contrite, or was he merely going through the motions to appease the Gods so to speak? I don't know. All I do know is that he was much pleasanter to be around and I let my guard down ever so slowly.

Within three months I was healed enough to return to my job and moved back to Massachusetts, to a new apartment and acquired a car. Along with my job I also resumed my affair with no guilt for at this point was at least divorced.

My time at home in my parents had changed me, it had reignited my interest in all things spiritual. Even though I was happy in my life I felt a lack. I had daily conversations with my mom which reinforced this feeling.

My parents had begun the process of building their property into a sustainable farm and I eagerly looked forward to my monthly visits there to catch up on all the progress as it was also something I aspired to have in my future too.

Less than a year after my sojourn at my parents' house for my healing my mother asked if I would be interested in moving back home to help with the farm. I told her I would think about it and get back to her within a week.

The very next day I found out that my apartment building was being sold for tax sale as the owner was very delinquent on his taxes and all tenants were told they had 60 days to vacate. Another non-coincidence steering me to a life decision.

Once again, my ex-husband arrived with friends to move me and my belongings back to home to start another chapter to my life.

CHAPTER 19

The Exchange

I arrived back home in the spring of 1996, just in time for planting season. My dad had started a new garden across the road in front of the house in addition to the acre garden we had always had up behind the house. As if that wasn't enough he also was using the garden space down at his parents' farm now belonging to his younger brother/cousin.

You guessed it, I was the main labor force, dad working two jobs, leaving him only the weekends to help. It was back breaking work and something I would not have been able to do at all a year ago. I was in awe everyday of the healing I had been given.

In addition to the garden's dad had built a barn for a milk cow so we could make our own butter and cheese and had several longhorn cattle for meat. I got a crash course in learning how to milk a cow when dad fell off the barn roof and broke his wrist.

I really liked gardening and took genuine pleasure in my accomplishment and watching things grow. But being a slave to the gardens did not garner me an income so I looked for a job. I found employment at a gas station and convenience market in town for the evening shift, a perfect counterpart to my daytime activities. I also applied at our local post office for the position of substitute postmaster with thoughts of a possible future fulltime career.

First memory: The application. The US postal service, though now an independent business, is run under federal guidelines and the application process is in depth to say the least. Applicants are required to record every job and place of residence from the time they were sixteen.

This process became a nightmare for me, for even though I had not had episodes of complete memory loss in a while, I had adopted a habit, when moving, of putting whatever had been going on where I had been living behind me and only concentrating on the present. Consequently, I had more than a difficult time remembering the where I had been and the what I had been doing. Between the ages of 18 and 36 I had over 15 addresses under my belt and more jobs than I could count.

Luckily for me, my mother, other relatives and friends had simply crossed out my previous addresses in their address books and written my new one underneath. Starting with my mom and asking her to check her address book was how I was able to fill in that part of the application. As for the jobs worked, I could match jobs to locations lived but not the time frames of those jobs, I just sort of winged it on start dates and end dates.

Apparently, I filled the application out sufficiently because I got the job. Once the application was submitted I had to take a civil service exam for postal workers(which I passed with flying colors with a near perfect score) I had to be finger printed, have an FBI background check and a physical. It took me two weeks, several hours a day just to fill out the application.

You would think I would have started keeping track of pertinent information after the struggle of trying to remember all that data, but no. As the years have rolled by and my life has gone on I still dismiss what was and concentrate on the now and future. In recent years the problem arising from this lack of keeping documentation has been my medical records, which are scattered all over the United States with me not remembering doctor's names, hospitals, dates of diagnosis or procedures.

Being determined not to let my past undermine my future, I put behind me, not only the bad but the good and useful. I find this rather strange or I should say a conundrum because I generally do everything in order like a recipe, follow the rules to the point of being anal, like in the writing of this book trying to keep it chronologically in order.

I had come to a point in my writing several chapters ago where I couldn't remember the exact chronological path things had taken. In my frustration I stopped writing, furious and disappointed in myself over my forgetfulness. For nearly three months I pouted and put myself down replacing the invisible sign my dad had placed around my neck with the words, "stupid" and "worthless" written on it, with a duplicate sign I had created myself.

Falling into that negative mindset was more comfortable for me than dealing with the issue that made it arise. In this case it was not being able to let go of the regimen that had been beat into me of proper procedure in matters of work or tasks. I am very free and spontaneous in my life except where anything work related is concerned, this is the way it is done and that's it!

In my writing I have not been able to stick to a strict chronological dialog, my memory loss making that impossible. To complicate that further as I am telling my tale I am releasing the caustic garbage that has been fermenting inside me, its poisonous discharge permeating all aspects of my life. The release of all that toxic rhetoric prompts return of even more memories allowing me to extract those forgotten bits and pieces of my life, good and bad that have been squished down and buried in darkness.

These missing pieces to my past do not surface in any order, appearing at random, traveling into the light along the path of the memories that came before. How to keep them chronologically in order without rewriting each chapter to place them where they properly belonged was driving me nuts making me mean, sick and self-hating.

It was only recently that I was able to recognize a pattern to these remembrances. The remembrances come about when writing about a situation and my way of dealing with that situation having been affected by an earlier trauma or circumstance. My spontaneous memories may not be in order time wise but are in logical order emotionally.

I had so much hatred and shame being released that I even created a smell for it, a smell that I detested, cigarette smoke. All I could smell for weeks was cigarette smoke, thick choking cigarette smoke, so real it stung my eyes and burned my throat. I felt like I was in a small unventilated room full of that stench.

I kept asking my husband, "do you smell it?"

"Am I being haunted by someone?"

"Why can't I get rid of it?"

Some days the smoke smell even followed me to bed, so irritating I could not fall asleep. On the nights it was so strong I had to burn a candle just to get some sleep.

It was not until visiting with a dear friend (another of my psyki-do-dah companions) that she helped me to realize that it was a self-made manifestation and upon immediately recognizing the truth of it the smoke disappeared.

That is until a few moments ago when the smoke made a reappearance, its presence compelling me to write about it, out of chronological step, offering me a new tune to dance and live my life by.

Second memory. Fanny Fuzzbutt. When I had been living at home a few years earlier hiding from my ex-boyfriend, I had opened my apartment door one day to the pitiful crying of a beautiful little kitty. She was a full-grown Manx cat but on the small side, covered in the most luxuriant yellow gold, long hair, yellow, not orange.

I wasn't supposed to have any pets but I couldn't help myself, it was love at first sight and she wouldn't leave. Waiting to choose a name I observed that she was always pulling the hair off her butt and would be staring at me with a mouthful of fluff. So, her name became Fanny Fuzzbutt, Fanny for short and when referring to her I always called her my butt-butt kitty.

Fanny had traveled with me here and there through both moves and here we were back again in the state where we had found each other. Manx cats are notorious for having poop problems. The genetic glitch that rendered them tailless also causing nerve problems in their hind quarters. Paralysis, partial paralysis and potty problems.

Fanny had problems having bowel movements aggravated by her not liking to drink. I had to force liquids with an eye dropper and offer extra moist food. I also had to cut glycerin suppositories into slivers and insert them into her rectum just so she could poop, her stools so dry she could not pass them.

Fanny had been my loving companion for three years at the time I was applying for the postal position. I had gone to my physical for the postal job and it was discovered I had a heart murmur. The doctor set me up with an appointment with a cardiologist for the following week as the murmur was quite pronounced.

I had set my furniture up in my parents' garage as it was heated and it offered me my own private space away from too much interaction with dad. Except for meals I spent all my free time in my garage apartment when dad was home.

Coming back into the garage after breakfast, several days after my physical, I found Fanny laying on the floor, eyes wide and glazed, breathing heavily. I rushed her to the vet where she was diagnosed with a class 4 heart murmur, her organs shutting down from lack of oxygen and proper blood flow. Heartbroken, I held her as she was put sleep by the vet.

The following week I go to my appointment at the cardiologist and my heart murmur has disappeared and my EKG is flawless. Did Fanny take my heart murmur onto herself? It hadn't been there previously. Had she sacrificed herself out of love for me because I had been so caring and attentive to her physical problem, which if it had gone unattended would have resulted in a painful death for her.

I believe she did. There are many remarkable, magical and mystifying stories of the love bonds between humans and their pets. I truly believe that Fanny took my heart murmur in thanks for giving her a happy, pain free life for three years. Her sacrifice allowing me to live without the restrictions imposed by a severe heart murmur.

This world is an amazing place and the bonds that many of us have shared with our animal companions are nothing short of miraculous. Even if you are someone who has never known the loving companionship of a pet if you put your mind to it, there is sure to be a memory of some kind of animal interaction that gave you pause.

A graceful bird in the sky drawing your attention, the antics of a squirrel creating a random smile, or seeing a child hug a dog in the park. They are here to let us know we are never alone and remind us to shed our seriousness for a moment and simply be.

CHAPTER 20

Alien Intervention

I stayed very busy that first summer, garden during the day, the convenience mart in the evenings and the odd day and Saturday mornings at the post office. I had always enjoyed working with the public, they were anonymous, not knowing the real me. I felt no shame or need to be other than who I was in my public jobs.

The only people I had difficulties with feeling lacking on many levels with was teenagers. When I had to deal with teenagers in my job I became the shy, hurt, woe begotten, scared teen I had been before. My adulthood melting off me like hot butter, feelings of panic and incompetence rising to the surface.

I felt like I was being judged and my heart would race in the few moments it took me to wait on them. The part of me that had been hurt back then still responded as that teenager and for many more years to come until only recently. I was clearly in my fifties before this conditioned response finally came to an end.

I was not home long before I learned the real reason for dad's determination for a sustainable lifestyle, it too was fear based. Both of my parents were into the earth changes craze running rampant in the 1990's, we all were. Dad had his focus on defending himself and his resources against the hoards that would be scavenging for survival. Along with stock piling food he was stock piling weapons.

I did not buy into the heavy threat theory just a sense to be prepared with essentials for a short period of time. I have never possessed that driving will to live. I know what awaits us on the other side and I would rather take myself out of the game then survive in destitution and pain.

Dad offered to teach me to shoot one of his semi-automatic rifles but I declined, a part of me still imagining killing him, I did not want to test the idea.

A girl I worked with at the convenience mart had a litter of kittens she was taking care of, the momma cat not particularly maternal. Knowing I had recently lost my Butt-Butt kitty she arrived to work one day carrying an adorable, fluffy, yellow kitten. If I had not known his birth date and Fanny's date of death I would have thought she had reincarnated to me through him. His fur was the exact shade of liquid sunshine that hers had been, alike in temperament, and also sporting golden eyes.

My heart melted on the spot and I took him home with me. In a word he was a hellion, he actually climbed the walls. I had no choice but to name him Trouble. Our love affair lasted 10 years.

It was a very hot summer and we all worried about the gardens and then a very peculiar thing happened.

First memory. A gift from the Gods. Feeling extraordinarily exhausted one night I fell into bed earlier than usual and immediately went to sleep. Falling asleep quickly is not something I had ever done easily. Even though I had received a great healing I still had pain associated with my back and bedtime is when it caught up with me. I had learned that if I kept going, kept in motion I could hold the pain at bay, but the minute I relaxed and quit moving everything seized up.

In my dreams that night I remember standing in a great grey expanse, high ceilings, long, wide corridors extending out in several directions. I stood there communicating with an odd little being. Communicating, not talking, we conversed with our minds, telepathy. He informed me his name was Orlok.

Orlok, was similar in appearance to the grey aliens that we have heard so much about; a bit taller, head not as elongated, complexion creamier colored than grey, and he was wearing a form fitting white jumpsuit.

He held a metal, devise in his hands maybe two and a half feet high and a foot long, the width only in inches. An arm of it sticking up at a steep angle reminding me of a grain elevator.

Orlok, went on to explain that he was going to place the device deep in the ground at our farm so that when all the farms around us succumbed to the imminent drought our gardens would be prolific.

I awoke the next morning in full memory of the encounter and raced into the house to tell mom. I grabbed a piece of paper and a pencil and tried to draw what I had seen, but I couldn't. I could see it in my mind but when I would try to put it to paper, it would become fuzzy, indistinct. I tried numerous times but apparently it was something that Orlok, and whomever, thought I was not to share at that time.

The fears of drought forecast for our region followed true and many farms and orchards in the area suffered great loss, but not us. Our gardens were like mini gardens of Eden. The plants were huge, many towering over my head, lush, thick, overloaded with fruits and veggies.

Dad had also planted some ancient grains to see how they would do. I recall the amaranth, as tall as me and the seed heads as large as my fist. It was amazing, the splendor of the gardens was all I needed to confirm that the communication I had with Orlok, was genuine.

For years I tried to draw the device from memory but it always evaded me. It was around 10 years later that I came upon the shape of the devise that Orlok had planted under our farm in the image on a book cover. I had been given a book written by Zechariah Sitchin, an author, who wrote about ancient civilizations. The picture on the cover of the book showed an image of the Great Pyramid at Giza, in which the front of the pyramid had been cut off showing the layout of the chambers and tubes inside.

I stood holding the book in shock, instantly recognizing the design of the inside of the pyramid. The devise Orlok showed me was an exact replica of the interior of the Great Pyramid, only in miniature. I was so excited and extremely curious to find more information about the pyramid.

Ancient civilizations already a subject I studied, it did not take me long to discover that many ancient civilization theorists believe that the pyramids around the earth were transmitters and conductors of energy.

I was astounded and in awe that something so magnificent had been shared with me, nobody.

The devise in my garden had to draw energy down to sustain our crops, for that is what happened. If it was identical to the one in the Great Pyramid, then that too must draw universal energy in, but what did it do with the energy after receiving it? It had to go somewhere didn't it? Does this prove/demonstrate that the pyramids around the earth are ancient energy stations?

My gut tells me yes but I am not qualified to make such an assumption. With a strong inner urging compelling me to share this information, after writing about this incident, I sent out 2 emails to different organizations that have been investigating alien interactions with humans. Will they think I am a crack-pot? Who knows, I did what I was compelled to do like I have done most of my life.

I remember enough to know that I had a few more meetings with Orlok, but there is only fog in my mind as to what they were about. Even though I have no concrete memory of the encounters, do I believe they occurred? Absolutely.

CHAPTER 21

A Date with Destiny

I was really enjoying my time at home, dad was still working two jobs which allowed my mother and me to share quite a bit of time together. I didn't have to go into work until 5 pm so after chores were done, mom and I had plenty of time to devote to our favorite psyki-do-dah ventures.

My mother was able to do energy healing and worked with a spiritual doctor, not in physical form called Dr. Jonah. My mother's healing abilities had increased dramatically since receiving her healing two years previously. Moms' hands would turn bright red and you could see waves of heat and energy emanating from them when she was around someone who needed healing.

First memory: Hot hands. One day my mom and I had gone to a grocery store in a neighboring town, not our small-town store where my mom knew nearly everyone who came through the door. The store and its customers were unfamiliar to us.

We are walking down an aisle browsing when my mother stopped, lifted her hands from the cart and stared at her hands.

She said, "I wonder who this is for?"

Moms' hands are bright red and zinging with energy, she looks up and only one other customer is in the aisle with us, a woman. Mom leaves the cart and walks over to the woman, a complete stranger, and says, "this must be for you." and just grabs the woman's arm before any explanation.

The woman is too shocked to say anything, her eyes like that of a deer caught in your headlights. I was completely embarrassed and even more afraid that the woman was going to yell for help and we would get arrested. I could feel a panic attack on the rise and flustered I just walked away. I went down the next aisle and hearing no screams for help I turned back up the aisle where my mother was and observed the woman crying with her hand on top of my mom's hand.

The woman was telling my mother that she had just recently been diagnosed with cancer and she was thanking my mother for approaching her saying that she had not even processed the idea of having cancer and had not told anyone about it yet. My mother's hands cooled down and I believe they exchanged phone numbers, leaving me even more embarrassed for being embarrassed.

I envied my mother's ability to be so open and unafraid with people. I was only like that at work for like an actor I assumed the role of clerk or post master. In private I hadn't invented a role for myself yet. Technically, in years I was an adult but the greater part of me was still the tormented child that responded to many situations with fear and an overwhelming feeling of worthlessness.

My mother sold Avon in her spare time, her outgoing personality and ease with people made her very successful at her job. Mom was so successful at her job that she won awards and proudly displayed them on a shelf in the dining room.

My mother always followed her intuition, (I guess I learned that from watching her) which led her to meeting people she was supposed to meet. I remember mom telling me about being at a customer's house delivering an order one day and she asked the woman if there was anyone that lived further along the road who might be interested in Avon. The woman told my mother that there was no one worth bothering with, only a few homes. When my mother left her customer's house she felt compelled to go down the road feeling there was someone she was supposed to meet and she did meet a woman who was an Avon addict but also needed healing as she was dying of colon cancer.

In her bi-monthly visits to the house at the end of the road mom became friends with the woman there Linda and her husband Zabriel. My mother told me when she first met Zabriel she recognized him as a fellow healer and told him so. A quiet, shy man Zabriel stepped into his role as healer in an instant. It was as if my mother had given him permission to assume his true identity. Once Zabriel had been told he could heal his inner being took over and he surpassed anyone in his abilities my mother had ever met among her metaphysical friends.

When I had been home convalescing from my back surgery I had gone with my mother on her Avon rounds one day and our last stop was at Linda's.

Second memory: A meeting with destiny. Arriving at Linda's house my mom and I were invited in and sat enjoying tea and conversation with her. This being the first and only time I met Linda, I was impressed by how up front and fearless she was concerning the state of her health, telling us of the problems she was having with her colostomy bag, the pains in her body from the treatments and her knowing the disease was spreading.

While sitting there her husband Zabriel came in from the barn and murmured hello to us, grabbed something and left again, the sum total of our first meeting less than 30 seconds. A few minutes later we got up to leave and Linda walked us to the door and stood on the porch as mom and I walked to the car. We were about halfway to the car when Linda called out and said, "Sophie would be good for Zabriel."

Linda waved and turned to reenter her house. Mom and I both heard what Linda had said but the impact of her words did not fully register until many months later. Linda had chosen me and given her blessing for Zabriel to become my future husband.

After Linda's passing, Zabriel became an unofficial member of the family, mom inviting him to holiday meals and weekend cook-outs. I had been down to my parents several times to visit in the year prior to moving back in 1996 for holidays and random visits and Zabriel was most always there.

Zabriel had a large family but no one that he could discuss his newly discovered spiritual abilities with or felt comfortable sharing his grief with except my mother. In time he was able to share with us his healing attempts on Linda. The cancer had metastasized and spread to various organs and John would zap a particular spot, the cancer would disappear only to pop up in another location, until eventually Linda, told him to stop healing her that it was her time to go.

I can't imagine how he felt knowing he had this great gift of healing and not being able to heal the one he loved. Like me it was his spiritual intuitiveness that got him through. There is a cycle to all life and a purpose in all life and sometimes that purpose is not to continue in life.

I was very aware of a deep connection with Zabriel on a spiritual level, the three of us, mom, Zabriel and I spending many hours in conversation and exploring our spiritual gifts. Surprisingly, dad too was interested and shared spiritual things that had happened to him and eagerly became interested in topics we were discussing.

I met a man at work in 1997 we started dating and we were several weeks into our relationship when he finally divulged he was still married. I just couldn't seem to catch a break from getting involved with gay or married men. I had to my misfortune been in relationships with three gay men and two married men. I often felt like I had a neon sign on my forehead that said, "try me until you figure out what you want to be!"

Third memory: Sex versus meat. Even though I now knew my current crush was married I did not end the affair. I really liked him and my mother liked him, who knew what could come of it. I wasn't in love with him but I so wanted someone in my life.

In anticipation of our evening together I had made homemade bread and beef barley soup for our dinner, it was a Friday night. When my date arrived, I offered him dinner and he wouldn't eat the soup as he was a supposed strict Catholic and did not eat meat on Fridays.

We shared some bread with wine in my garage apartment and before long we were in bed having sex. Later that night after he left, my mom was still awake watching a program on television and I went in and sat with her, laughingly telling her about my date refusing meat but willing to commit adultery. I mean as far as sin goes in the Catholic faith I'm thinking adultery is much higher up on the list than eating a little meat!

The disregard he paid his religion only highlighted how low I was on his list of priorities and I knew then I would only ever be a convenient piece of ass to him. The affair ended that night, though I did see him at the store once in a while.

When I wasn't working I took my meals with my parents and as the months rolled by I was able to see the developing cruel nature of their relationship more clearly. With only mom left in the house dad had taken his penchant for belittling someone out on my mother. He talked down to her and had begun using the self-esteem busting rhetoric on her that he had used on me. Mom would just sit there and take it, in anger, I would get up from the table mid meal and go out to my space.

The response I got from mom when asking her why she stayed with him was always the same, "I love this house and this land and only death will make me leave it."

Fourth memory: Follow the signs: Coming home one day after a morning shift I walked in on my mother frantically searching through a pile of newspaper clippings. With tears in her eyes she told me she was looking for a recipe that dad had cut out of the newspaper and given her so she could make it.

Mom had lost the recipe and had stalled dad off for a week in excuses on why she did not make it but he had gotten very belligerent to her on the phone that day demanding she make it. I told her to just wing it for she knew the basic ingredients and dad would not know any better as he had never had it before.

After making the salad mom and I were sitting in the living room and she turned to me and said, "I don't know how much longer I can put up with him he is driving me crazy.

Fifth memory: The second sign: Me and mom had gone to the hairdresser so we could both get our hair cut. The beautician was another of our spiritual friends and also a gifted medium. As mom was walking in the door to the beauty shop she did a little dance and announced, "I'm not going to color my hair anymore I finally get to be who I really am."

We three talked about many things and at one point in the conversation the hairdresser looked at me and asked, "who's Zabriel, I see his energy all around you?"

I told her we were friends and the memory of what Linda had said came bubbling up to the surface of my subconscious and I shared that with her too. When mom and I were leaving she told me she would see me soon but did not say that to my mother.

Sixth Memory: The third sign. My mother had a mild heart attack some 5 or 6 years earlier and had been on several heart medications since then. Arriving home after a doctor visit one day mom made a big production of announcing she no longer needed any of her medications. This information did not ring true for me, I couldn't imagine any doctor stopping that kind of medicine cold turkey but there it was. I am pretty sure mom decided all on her own to stop taking it.

Sixth memory: The saddest day of my life. On February 12, 1998, I came in from my apartment and mom was sitting in dad's chair looking ashen with her right hand laying across her chest and asked me to call the ambulance. After making the call mom turned to me and said, "I don't mean to leave you but I can't live with him anymore and I don't expect you to take care of him."

Luckily my cousin was a first responder and living next door so he was there in minutes, taking vitals and keeping her calm while awaiting the ambulance. Mom was transported to our local hospital about 15 miles away, where dad was employed as a bio-medical technician. It was a small hospital and did not offer a full cardiac department, they spent hours trying to stabilize her before sending her to the bigger fully equipped hospital some 20 minutes away.

In a brief moment before they transported her, mom called me into the room and told me the pin number to their bank card, dad not knowing it because mom handled all the finances. It was the last thing she ever said to me and I have used that number for various accounts ever since.

Mom was transported and immediately taken into the O.R. for a stent placement and the blood clot removed. While in recovery barely conscience she mumbled a question to no one in particular, "will I be able to work in my garden?"

I was not near her only standing in the doorway, her eyes were closed, I do not think it was any earthly being she was talking to. The doctor told dad and I that she would be out of it until the next day, that we should go get something to eat and get a good night's sleep.

We left never having spoken to her and made our way to the pay phones in the lobby to let the family know what had happened and from there started towards home stopping at a restaurant only minutes from the hospital. We had just gotten our food when I had an overwhelming urge to call the hospital. I got up from the table and went to the pay phone and called. My gut feeling was right, the hospital had been trying to get a hold of us and asked us to return to the hospital immediately.

We were greeted at the door of the CCU with sad faces and escorted into a room where we told mom had passed away just moments after we had left. A ventilator had been left in even though she was DNR because she was an organ donor.

The doctor told us mom had started hemorrhaging as her blood pressure began rising after surgery. The blood clot had deprived the front part of her heart of blood for too long and the heart tissue had disintegrated under the pressure of the renewed flow.

Walking like a zombie with dad following I made my way to the lobby and started calling family back that were in the process of getting ready to come see mom in the hospital and instead would be coming to her funeral. I managed all that without a tear falling.

Dad and I rode back to the other hospital where my car was and I told him I would be home directly. In the privacy of my car I drove down the road sobbing and yelling at my mother for leaving me all alone in the world, that I wasn't ready for her to leave me yet.

Hoarse of voice and dripping with snot and tears I made it home where dad was sitting in his chair crying. Passing by he grabbed me and pulled me to him laying his head against my stomach and sobbing what was he going to do without her. I could not have cared less, all I wanted to do was go out to my room and call Zabriel.

In the weeks following mom's death, when looking back over the past six months, the signs that she was preparing to leave stood out. Wanting her hair long and silver like her grandmother, not caring about her appearance. Becoming who she really was, a spiritual being. Stating she didn't think she could live with dad anymore and lastly quitting her medication.

This was my first time recognizing the sequence of events leading up to a person leaving this world, since then I have witnessed these subtle leave takings numerous times.

Today's society has drifted far from our spiritual roots, addicted to our drama and media we have all but lost our ability to perceive the simple and subtle messages around us. The quiet and unobtrusive nuances of change lost in the often harsh and chaotic environment in which we have become adapted to.

CHAPTER 22

Orphan

When my mother left this life, she took every ounce of her being with her. There was no lingering sense of her ever having lived in that house. Typically, when someone passes there is some residual energy of that person left behind, a hint of perfume, cologne, or feeling if you walk into the next room they will be there.

The house was dead, as if it had never enjoyed any life within its walls. There was no lingering odor of her perfume, or life force. Mom's energy had brightened our home making it a place where everyone wanted to gather in spite of dad. When mom died it was more than her I lost, I lost the extended family too.

Mom had been the glue that had held the family together, a beacon of light around which the entire family and friends fluttered. Aunts, uncles and cousins near and far no longer had that communal gathering place and retreated into their own secular, immediate family units. I felt an orphan.

After the funeral, I spent the next 2 weeks helping dad sort mom's things, figure out the bills and teach him how to use the washing machine, something he hadn't done in 30 years. That done I figured I didn't owe him anything else and moved out into an apartment only a few miles from my place of work.

I liked my new apartment, a large open loft style place originally a barn workshop, towering ceilings and open wood beams. I had the whole upstairs to myself, oh and my cat Trouble too. I took much joy in his companionship, his antics lighting my heart.

First memory: Squirrel. I was sitting in my apartment one day quietly reading a book when Trouble went flying by me in a flash of gold knocking everything off the end table, ricocheting off the wall and up the beam. It took me a moment to notice he was in pursuit of a flying squirrel.

The only thing Trouble saw was squirrel, there was mass destruction in his wake. He leapt from any surface he could that would get him airborne to follow the flying rodent. The squirrel finally came to a standstill, I'm sure of pure exhaustion, on the back of the bathroom door. I was able to scoop it into a bowl with a lid and set it free outside.

Surveying my apartment afterwards it looked like a tornado had gone through the place. There were 2 broken lamps, broken dishes, every surface, tables and counter completely bare. If I didn't know better I could have sworn that my cat had sprouted wings.

In those first months after mom died I needed humorous incidents to help alleviate some of my grief. Even in the years that I lived hundreds of miles away I talked to my mother every day, if she didn't call me I called here. My first thought after rescuing the squirrel was to pick up the phone and tell her about it. Twenty years later, now and then, I still feel the impulse to pick up the phone.

The universe is a funny thing, we set so much up for ourselves before coming into life. I wondered if we set up these moments of pure ridiculousness in advance too or if they are gifts from our angels and loved ones on the other side? Either way, they are as necessary as the air we breath and the food we eat.

Like flowers capturing the first rays of sunshine and opening to it, laughter bubbles up inside us and opens us up to receive. Even if you are in a place or situation that is dark and depressing, think of how you feel when you open up to pure laughter. When the laughter ends there is a moment when you experience contentment and peace. Sometimes that split second of joy is enough to save you.

Second memory: The cook out. I was friends with my land lady and she had invited me to go to a Memorial Day cook out with her, I didn't have to be to work until 5 pm so I said I would go with her as long as we were back in time for me to make it to work on time. Shelia, drove and we arrived at her friend's house out in the country a lush green place with towering trees.

She parked the car and we went up to the patio area adjacent to the house and deposited our dish to pass among all the others. We made a brief stop in the house to say hello to our host who told us to help ourselves to a bite to eat and then come over to the pool area where everyone was congregating.

We fixed our plates and attempted to converse with the only other people on the patio, they merely nodded and continued to quickly shovel food in their mouths, then abruptly got up and hurried to the pool like they were being chased by bees. My, "this is kinda weird meter" clicked on about then alerting me of things to come.

Finishing our food, we started out across the lawn, a path of stepping stones leading the way. Shelia's eye sight was not that good so she was walking with her head down to watch her step, unfortunately, I was looking straight ahead.

Approaching us from the pool area was a completely naked man, slight of build and maybe 5 ft. 7 in. tall, his most impressive feature was his enormous shlong! I kid you not, it was like an elephant trunk, swaying and slapping against his thighs as he walked, the head nearly reaching his knees. I knew then that I better prepare myself for whatever I was to witness once we entered the enclosed pool area, engrossed in watching her step Shelia never saw Moby Dick.

When we arrived at the pool area Shelia, raised her head and said, "I forgot to tell you they're nudists"

I replied, "I think I figured that out a way back"

We stood in the opening of the pool enclosure and my eyes were seared by the amount of white flesh glistening in the sun. I was not then nor am I now prejudice against anyone for their religion, color or size. I had for most of my life been over weight and got ridiculed for it but to see that much bare flesh with no warning took my breath away. There was three women in the pool each weighing in excess of 400 lbs. each. There was every shape and size of human you could ever imagine and all naked.

Our host was at the far end of the pool area sitting at a table with an umbrella and we had to make our way to him across a row of naked bodies stretching the distance laid out on beach towels. Gingerly, stepping over outstretched legs we made our way to the back, half-way there I had to step over a man who was slathering sunblock on his balls.

Finally arriving at our hosts table, we exchanged small talk for a bit before making our goodbyes, explaining we had to leave as I had to go to work. We then had to turn and wade our way back through the sea of flesh.

I managed to contain myself the ride home but as soon as I got into my car to head to work I lost it! I laughed so hard that tears ran down my face and I started talking out loud to my mother saying, "you should have warned me, before I went." Looking into my rear-view mirror as if I expected her to be sitting there laughing with me. My co-workers enjoyed the story and I enjoyed telling it but I do not think it is an experience I would ever care to repeat.

I had remained in contact with Zabriel, talking with him on a daily basis. If John didn't call me I called him. My mother's death proved a catalyst in moving our relationship beyond friendship. If my mother hadn't died, I don't think he would have declared his feelings for me so quickly, he was and is a gentleman. I knew there was something between us but I always had a sense that he thought it would be rude or infringe upon his and my mother's friendship if he pursued me. I never asked him that, it is just what I felt.

We spent as much time together as we could between our respective jobs. I knew he loved me but I also knew he was holding back for some reason. I talked to him about moving in with him at his farm, but he would not answer me. Even when I came to the decision that I could not afford to stay in my apartment, he still did not ask me to move in with him.

In anger and frustration, I told him I was moving in with a guy friend I knew from work, a diabetic who needed someone to help take care of him. I had never been around a severe diabetic and it was brutal watching as he lost piece after piece of himself to amputations. Our arrangement was my assistance in exchange for a place to live.

I did not talk to Zabriel for a month or more but I loved him so much it was like surviving without sunshine. Eventually I went and saw him and he had missed me just as much. Staying with my friend had become very difficult for me the ups and downs of his blood sugar causing him to have violent mood swings with him screaming and yelling at me.

The yelling triggered flashbacks of dad and I became depressed and suicidal, one day taking nearly everything I owned, I put it in a pile in the back yard and set fire to it, symbolic of getting rid of myself. I again asked Zabriel if he would let me come live with him but he still would not let me.

Third memory: Here I go again. Unhappy and poor, I decided to go back to Massachusetts again where I could make a decent living. It was just after the first of the year of 1999 that I went back north. I had just gotten settled in my new apartment and rented furniture when I was struck with a pang of guilt about dad being alone for Easter.

I was a couple of hours into my trip home to spend Easter with dad, when the "voice of no reason" made its reappearance. The words felt like a breeze coming from behind me and it said, "you have to move to California."

I looked into the rear-view mirror as if I was talking to a real person and spoke rather loudly, "are you fucking kidding me? I just got settled."

The voice replied with, "you have to be there by the end of August"

I was shocked to silence, but my head was already planning on how I was to accomplish such a feat in four months.

I don't remember sleeping at dad's house all I remember is the next day dad telling me how proud he was to have had prolonged sex with his girlfriend (the same woman he had been having an affair with while my mom was alive) saying he didn't think he had it in him. I was completely repulsed, the whole conversation, not something any father should ever have with his daughter. Any guilt or sense of responsibility I thought I had concerning him wiped out in an instant. I got back in my car and drove back to Massachusetts, hate and loathing coursing through my veins better than any caffeine I could consume to keep me awake.

When I got back to New Hampshire, I called my sister and told her about the voice telling me to move out to California at the end of

First Memory

August. My sister like me, never questioned spiritual promptings and pretty much said, "ok."

The very next day I called the rental company and told them to come and take the furniture. In my living room I had my television on a box and a lawn chair to sit on, in the bedroom I had a pile of blankets to sleep on and a couple of totes for my clothes. For the better part of five months I lived like this saving every dime so I could leave at the designated time.

The end of August rolled around in the blink of an eye it seemed. I left my job a little before the end of the month so I could stop back home for a visit and still allow travel time to California and be there by the designated date. I had the same knack with traveling that I had with cooking always being able to judge how long something took to get done. On long trips I could guesstimate almost to the minute that I would get there.

Back home I had a goodbye luncheon with Zabriel and friends. All through lunch I could feel Zabriel's love and energy all around me and I felt for sure that he would ask me to stay with him. Lunch over I lingered over goodbyes, still waiting. Nothing. I got down to the end of the road, before turning onto the highway and sat there and cried, my tears keeping time with the gentle rain falling on my windshield.

Even though I was heartbroken, I took a deep breath and pulled out onto the highway. No matter what, I always heeded the voice. The voice never came without a prearranged reason and even though I did not know the reason I was going to California, I knew from past experience the purpose would reveal its self at the right time.

CHAPTER 23

Land of Sunshine

I have no memory of my drive to California, but I do know that I arrived on the day I had been told to get there by. Except for brief visits, one a family reunion when we all went out to California, a trip mom and I took to visit my sister while I was still living in New England and of course mom's funeral I had not spent quality time with my sister in 20 years.

My sister and I spent hours talking, strengthening our bond not only as sisters but as spiritual compatriots. The more time we spent together the more our abilities grew and our awareness of them. I was not alone, a part of John, had come with me, his love and protective energy surrounding me.

My sister had a son and daughter, now teenagers, much to my lament. I still had issues dealing with teenagers, even at 39 years old I felt all the old insecurities where they were concerned rising to the surface. I was so uneasy and fearful that I often came off as bitchy to them even though I loved them.

My sister was a wonderful mother and so easy with her kids, able to take part and enjoy the things they were interested in. But not me, even as a child I was old, never fitting in amongst my peer group. I felt awkward, stupid and at a total loss at how to participate.

In desperation I turned to my comfort zone which was to cook. I cooked huge family meals which no one had time to eat and frankly they were not used to the kind of home cooked meals that I made. I was used to following my mom's example of cooking hearty meals for people who did strenuous outside work, in the country, on top of holding down a 40+ hour a week job. I know I wasted a lot of money on food that no one ate but I could not stop myself, it was the only way I knew how to fit in, feel useful and confident.

I found work quickly in a circuit board shop just minutes from my sisters, my experience in that field making the job hunt fast and painless. I took the job even though I felt that I would not be there long, already one of my, "knowing's" giving me a sense that I would be leaving around the new year.

The reason for my move made itself known about three weeks after I got there, just like in all my previous moves. My sister had to have back surgery, the same surgery that I had several years earlier and I was there to help her. I knew everything she would be going through, I was perfect for the job. I also had a car that was not a low sporty model, that she could get into and out of with ease.

First memory: Healing old wounds. My sister's surgery may have been the impetus that set the timing of my move in motion but it was not the only reason I was supposed to be there. In looking back I see many reasons. Gayle and I had only ever had days, at most a week to spend in each other's company and my time there allowed us to really bond. Our earlier bond had been severed so abruptly by our parent's divorce that it left me with no memory and my sister with overwhelming guilt and sadness. It was a healing time for both of us.

Before my sister had been taken away she too had fallen victim to dad and our cousin. Even though she had no choice in leaving she felt she had abandoned us, my brothers and I to dads' abuse, a false guilt she carried even into adulthood. Living in a house with teenagers forced me to deal with emotions from my own childhood and lastly, I learned to play a little.

Second memory: Protection. Not really knowing how to act around teens and often saying the wrong thing, I inadvertently insulted my niece's boyfriend at the time. We were and are a family of power and high spiritual energy and my niece and nephew were no exception.

We are Lightworkers and light attracts dark. My niece's then boyfriend was also powerful and fell into dark energy when provoked.

In his anger at whatever I had said he launched an all-out negative energy attack against me. It was during that onslaught against me I found out just how strong Zabriel's love for me and his spiritual strength was.

I was not the only one to witness it, there were several of us fending off the negative energy when Zabriel's winged spiritual self, rose up behind me, wings spread and holding aloft a golden sword. The dark and swirling energy dissipating into sparkles like fireflies when confronted with the golden light emanating from the sword. It was at that point in my life the most wonderous thing I had ever beheld. Alone I might have thought it a figment of my imagination but my sister and niece witnessed it too.

Along with nursing my sister in her recovery from her back surgery I helped her fill in the void created when she was taken from mom. We spent long hours talking about our mother, me telling her about the mom I knew and her telling me about the mom I couldn't remember. There were many aspects about mom that overlapped each other's telling's but like me there were noticeable differences before and after the trauma.

Oddly enough, I do not feel anger or hatred towards my mother concerning the abuse I suffered. I've wondered at that, thought hard and actually tried to summon up anger against her. I mean I really tried to force it so I could process it and put it behind me, but it just wasn't there. I think I identified with mom's victim status and her inability to come to terms with it.

I believe my mother kept all her anger, hate, fear and sadness bottled up inside her, until it consumed her and she willed herself to die. This too was one of the reasons I had to be with my sister, for us to share and release our traumas so we would not follow in our mother's footsteps and die way too young.

CHAPTER 24

Ancient Energies and Forgiveness

My sister on the mend and no longer needing my help, I felt the pull for a new adventure. I had, since the beginning of December, felt drawn to New Mexico. My mother's friend Olivia that she had known since her college days was living there in Taos.

Olivia, along with being one of my mother's closest friends had been a member of the spiritual group my mother attended. After my mother's death I kept in touch with her on a regular basis. Olivia was a retired college professor and writer of educational books for teachers, extremely spiritual, she became drawn to the mystery surrounding the Native American petroglyphs and people.

In the last days of December, I left for Taos, with the feeling that I had to be there for the first day of the new year 2000. I felt a change beginning within myself and for some yet unknown reason knew the metamorphosis would not be complete until I was there.

Olivia was like family, in fact when we were out and about we referred to each other as aunt and niece. It did not take me long to fall in love with all the ancient sites in the surrounding areas and the petroglyphs, god, how I loved the petroglyphs.

The job market in Taos was pretty much non-existent, I put applications in everywhere I could find, but it was still nearly 3 months before I landed a job. The time of my unemployment was not wasted for even though Olivia was always busy writing or revising her books we spent many long weekends exploring and discovering energy spots in Native American sites and National parks.

During our pilgrimage throughout the four corners region (New Mexico, Utah, Colorado and Arizona) I developed a new gift. I was able to connect to the residual energy left by the former inhabitants of these ancient sites. When I stood upon a Native American site or stood before a panel of petroglyphs I would feel a tingling energy flow up through me and it was as if a movie projector started running in my head and I could see what had happened there and I would narrate it to Olivia.

For those of you who do not know what residual energy is, I will try to explain by example. Have you ever walked by, stood on or driven by an area that gave you the shivers, made you feel sad or scared? Everything in this world is some form of energy from the ground under your feet to the tiniest hair on your head. These energies over a period of time begin to comingle and we leave traces of ourselves there. The energy in these spots of previous high population call tell a story to someone who is intuitive enough to hear or see it.

Places where battles have been fought and many have lost their lives are well known for the negative, sad energy that remains there. Look at businesses that have been built on a particular spot but no one seems to make a go of it, one after another until eventually the building is left abandoned often thought of as haunted. Most often it is not the building but the ground that is the cause the leftover energy of a tragedy or battle trapped there.

Every town has one of those buildings or places where something always feels off. Like an exorcism people of good intent and healing energy can help release this trapped energy. It is not just negative energy that can be felt, there are areas which we are drawn to that make us feel good, happy, content, sacred spots throughout time.

I felt so very blessed to be able to be drawn to these energy spots and to see and hear their story.

First memory: The cliff dwellings. I'll never forget my visits to the cliff dwelling sites, although I loved them all I felt a particular bond with Hovenweep National monument in Utah. A firm believer in reincarnation I truly felt I had once lived there and its story tugged at my heartstrings.

There are many common threads that link all the ruins of the southwest, one of the foremost being the craftsmanship of the buildings. The evidence of their building ability represented by so many of the structures still existing today. The fact that these early peoples were such great craftsmen is one of the reasons for the building of the nearly inaccessible cliff dwellings and for the disappearance of the people who had lived there.

Hovenweep, has a series of watch tower ruins and as I stood before one on my first visit there it was as if I was inside the tower and the story unfolded before my eyes. The sequence of events that I was given showed a sentry atop the tower watching the south and spotting a signal fire. In the back of my mind and his mind for now we were linked I knew that there were a series of signal fires on high spots stretching all the way to Mexico. The fires signaled invaders from the south approaching. The sentries gave the warning and runners were sent to the outlying communities to spread the message raiders coming.

The scene fast forwarded to show hundreds being captured and taken to the south of Mexico where they became skilled craftsman slave labor forced to build the great temples there. The cliff dwellings were an attempt at hiding themselves and making themselves inaccessible to the slave traders.

I saw the once large population of these early Native people dwindle over the course of the years to these regular raids. Eventually, the raids coupled with the long years of drought in that region forced those remaining natives to abandon their dwellings in search of more fertile lands and smaller communities so as not to deplete the resources.

I shook my head as if coming out of a daze and felt a stream of tears gliding down my face. Over the years I made several pilgrimages to Hovenweep and each time I was struck with the same gentle sadness. When the Lord of the Rings, movies came out, each time I watched the scene in which the signal fires are lit requesting aid I would cry, just like I did at Hovenweep.

As much as I loved the various ruins I loved the petroglyphs and pictographs even more, many of the glyphs I did not understand but some I recognized immediately and was able to identify. With my history of UFO and alien interaction I was most keenly drawn to the images depicting the star visitors.

When I was around the petroglyphs I felt so alive and energized, with the aid of my walking stick I scrambled over the rocks like a mountain goat. Olivia would give me her camera and I would hike and climb to the more difficult spots and take pictures for her, also carrying my own camera and using it too. Even on unmarked trails I had a knack for finding the ancient artwork.

Whenever I came upon a rock depicting "presumed" extraterrestrials (for many scholar's poo-poo the idea all together) I felt the truth of it and its importance. I firmly believe that star visitors were here, some are still here and that they will have a significant role in our future.

The Native American lore concerning their connection to the Sky People led us to visit several areas where it has been rumored there are, have been, and still are, underground extraterrestrial bases.

Second memory: Angel Peak. One of the sites rumored to have been an underground base is Angel Peak, New Mexico. When we visited there, I felt a deep connection not so much to the site but to the race that had lived there. Maybe I had, in a previous life, been one of these star people I could picture in my mind, or maybe I was again just picking up the residual energy there.

I saw a race of tall, slender, blue skinned beings that had lived in an underground colony there long before Native peoples lived in that area. They were kind, gentle and had used their intelligence and technology to calm the seismic activity in the area before the influx of man.

I watched, in sadness, the story unfolding in my head, of these gentle visitors being overrun and killed by another race of star beings, come here to plunder the resources of this planet that the blue aliens had been preserving.

Third memory: Forgiveness. From the moment I started visiting all those strong energy centers I could feel my humanness opening up to the more spiritual me. Not a day went by that I did not receive some sort of spiritual enlightenment. I felt the hatred I had harbored inside me towards my dad melt away to be replaced by pity for him. I came to understand that holding onto that hate was keeping that ugliness inside me, holding me back from becoming more.

When you hold onto hate and dwell on who it is directed towards it only eats at you it does not affect them, so why keep it? When you release hate, it is the ultimate victory over your abuser, for their joy was in keeping you down. At first it feels like the most impossible thing you could do. Hatred has become your baby, you have nurtured it, watched it grow, but it is a parasite.

What is a parasite? It is an organism that attaches itself to another living thing sucking its life force from it. Don't give up your life to a dark soul-sucking parasite of hatred, cut its roots and step away from its shadow into the light.

I sat in the sunshine with pen and paper in hand and wrote a letter to my dad forgiving him for all he had done to me. I told him there was no vengeance on this earth that I could direct towards him that could make up for what he had put me through. I told him that when he left this life and stood before God or whatever higher power he believed in and his soul reviewed the deeds of his life he would suffer unimaginable pain. I told him I felt pity for what he would have to atone for, feeling it would be greater than any punishment he would have suffered here. Then I mailed it.

I believe it is important to write it, there is power in the written word, but I do not think it is necessary to mail it. Once written it can be burned and released and the new parasite free you can rise from the ashes.

Forgiveness is not easy it took me 40 years and when I sat down to finally put it in writing I did not picture the physical face of dad and all the negativity attached to it. Instead I pictured just a tiny pinprick of light, that spark of creation in all of us, unsullied by the human experience.

My greatest wish is that in the reading of my story you have discovered the spark inside you that can become the flame of the whole you, banishing the darkness. Blessings.

CHAPTER 25

Endings Welcome Beginnings

The release of hatred with the mailing of the letter gave me a sense of peace that I had never felt before in my life. I had not realized just how heavy the burden of hate was that I had carried for so long, I physically felt lighter and my eyes were brighter.

I had not known then the effect that negative emotions had on the physical body. There is much information out there now on how depression can cause and aggravate diseases in the body, hypertension, heart disease, diabetes to name but a few. Not having heard too much about that effect at that point in time I was surprised and perplexed at the physical changes that were happening to me.

First memory: Blindness. A few days after mailing the letter I awoke to total blindness, I could not open my eyes, try as I might. I called out for Olivia who upon entering my room exclaimed, "Oh my God, what happened?"

My eyes were completely glued shut with gunk, I could not even pry them open. There was at least a quarter inch crust covering each eye. Dressing herself then helping me to get dressed she took me to the medical clinic, guiding my steps with her hand on my arm.

The doctor said it was conjunctivitis, actually he said it was the worst case of it he had ever seen. I couldn't work, couldn't drive, could barely see for almost 2 weeks. The stuff just kept coming out, I had to wash my eyes of the crud several times a day with warm compresses and add ointment.

My eyes were not the only thing affected, my ears drained, my nose ran, I had an unusual vaginal discharge and my body smelled of old sweat. My hair became greasy something it had never been, always having dry hair. I got pimples, also something I never had even as a teen and I cried. I cried at the drop of a hat, with no warning or apparent trigger the tears came, by the bucket load.

I had shut myself down emotionally for so many years and never allowed myself to give into tears feeling that if I gave into, (to my way of thinking) that weakness I would lose control. Not feeling is how I coped.

It was if every bad thing I had ever seen, heard, felt and not expressed, released its self from my body. The purge lasted about 2 weeks and with the help of my metaphysical friends the reason for it explained. In my unwillingness and inability to release the trapped emotions and thoughts from my childhood, I had manifested them into a solid matter, a toxic goo so to speak.

I can't say the process of releasing was pleasant, it gave me new insight and understanding as to why many never finish the process of releasing. My advice, tough it out, the end result is well worth the pain.

After only 5 months with Olivia I knew the reason for being there had been accomplished. This time instead of spirit sending me to help someone else, I had been guided to a place where I could save me. With a feeling of hope and Zabriel's love on the horizon I turned towards home.

Arriving once again to my home turf I had a joyful reunion with Zabriel who was now able to tell me that, even though it broke his heart to let me go, his spirit guides had told him not to hold me back that I needed to make the journey.

Although we loved each other there were still some issues that Zabriel was dealing with in his family, so to keep the bills paid I went to Massachusetts for work and visited him every month. A year after returning from New Mexico, I went and got Zabriel and moved him to Massachusetts with me.

We had a glorious 6 months alone but then the "voice" urged us to return to his farm to discover there our new journey. We arrived home in November 2001 and were married on December 21, 2001in a small private ceremony. Seventeen years later we still love each other as much now as we did then, even more.

IN MEMORY, OF

Elliot, my brother. A gentle soul to brief upon this earth but forever in my heart.

My mother, who laid the foundation of my spiritual path with books and open-mindedness, instilling in me the curiosity to always want to discover more...

Printed in the United States
By Bookmasters